PHOTOGRAPHING CH

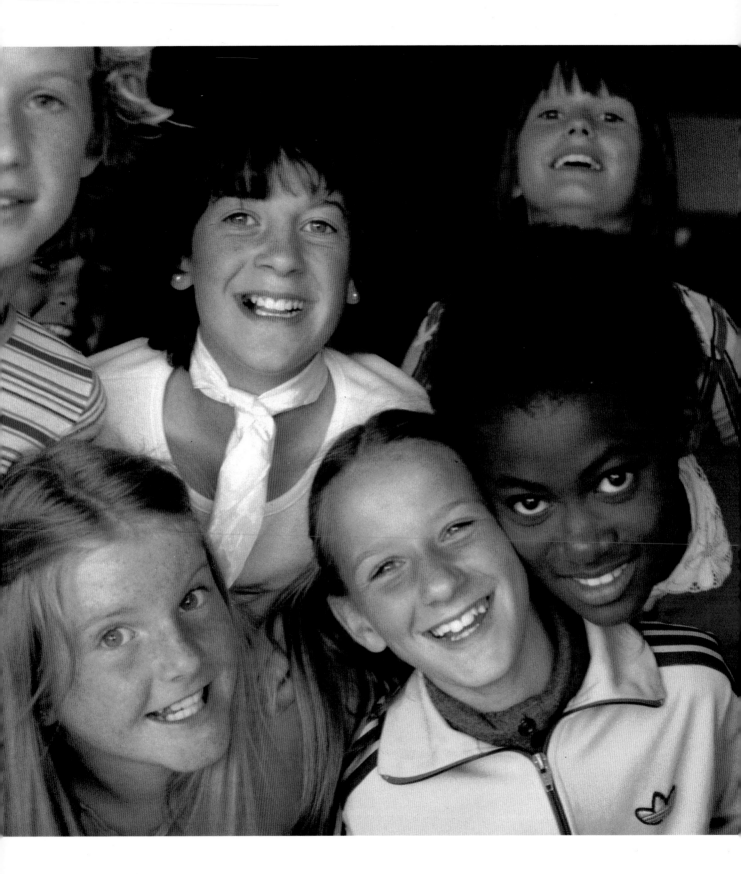

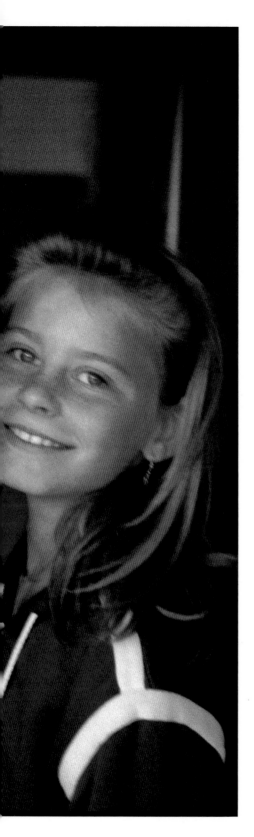

PHOTOGRAPHING CHILDREN

SUZANNE SZASZ

AMPHOTO
An Imprint of Watson-Guptill Publications/New York

Editorial Concept by Marisa Bulzone
Edited by Liz Harvey
Designed by Bob Fillie
Graphic Production by Ellen Greene

Copyright © 1987 by Suzanne Szasz

First published 1987 in New York by AMPHOTO,
an imprint of Watson-Guptill Publications,
a division of Billboard Publications, Inc.,
1515 Broadway, New York, NY 10036

Library of Congress Cataloging in Publication Data
Szasz, Suzanne.
  Photographing children.

  Includes index.
  1. Photography of children. I. Title.
TR681.C5S93 1987   778.9'25   87-11357
ISBN 0-8174-5469-1
ISBN 0-8174-5470-5 (pbk.)

Manufactured in Japan

1 2 3 4 5 6 7 8 9/93 92 91 90 89 88 87

*This book is dedicated
to the parents who allowed me
to photograph their children.*

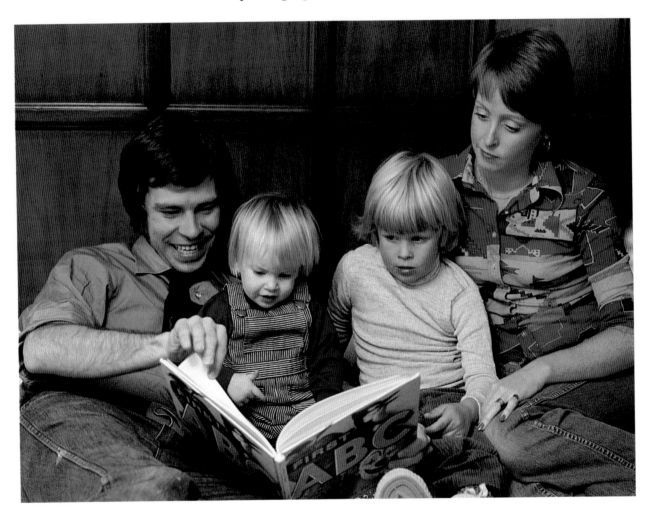

CONTENTS

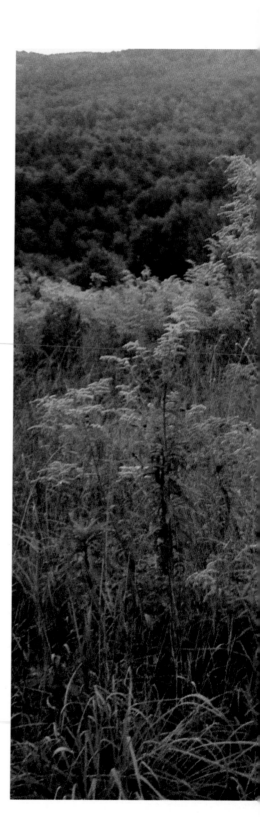

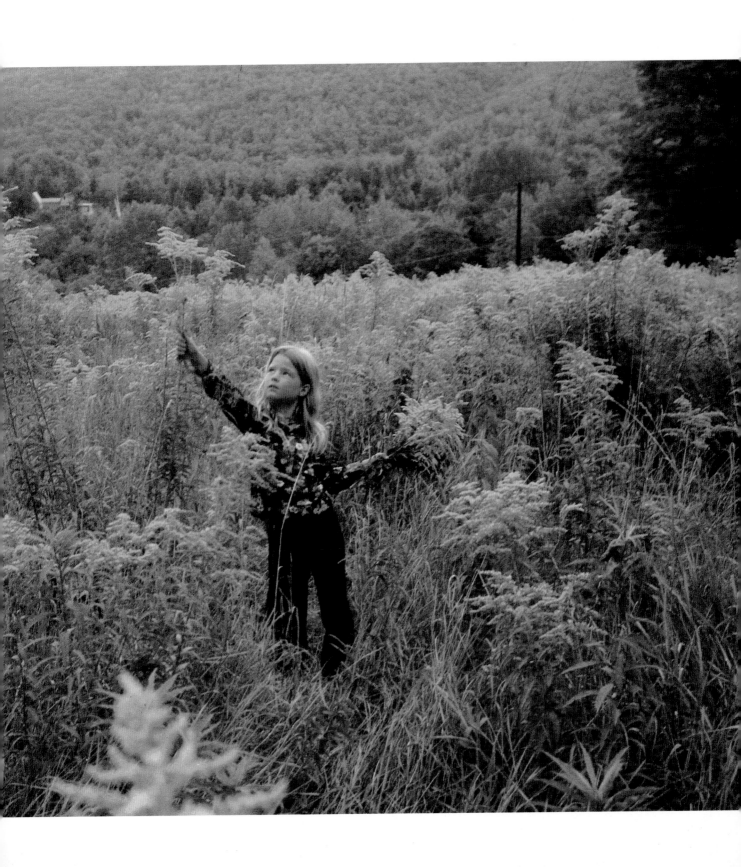

INTRODUCTION: THE BASICS OF PHOTOGRAPHING CHILDREN

I hope you are reading this book because you are enthusiastic about photographing children. Perhaps you have even become aware that you have a special bond with them.

That's what happened to me. I started photographing relatively late in life, after I had accepted that I was not going to have children of my own. I was immediately drawn to them as subjects, and soon realized that I had found the ideal substitute for what I was missing. Since then I have spent most of my time working with children. I frequently followed up my original assignment and went back to see how the children had grown.

You, too, must have a good reason for being attracted to photographing children; this enthusiasm will lead you to produce good work. Besides the usual rewards of discovering more and more about your field, you will benefit in another way: you will learn about *being* a child. Because we forget nearly everything about our first years, it is exciting to observe children and to relive this important time.

FIRST CONSIDERATIONS

Your Camera. Today's automated cameras can boggle the mind. But I think they can help you to simplify your photography if you know what they are capable of. You should understand such simple concepts as the effect of a fully open versus a closed-down diaphragm or the uses of differential focusing.

Do you think that a typewriter-computer that automatically corrects your spelling is the best way to learn your language? I hope not. I would rather learn to spell—mostly by trial and error—and know how to consult a dictionary.

So, by all means, get some of the new superstar cameras, but don't expect them to do your job. Be sure to make tests that show the result of letting the camera do everything and compare them to what you get when *you* decide on the lens opening and/or exposure time. After you have done such tests, try to develop speed and facility, which will often be better than will fussing endlessly in quest of perfection.

As *New York Times* critic Andy Grundberg recently noted, "Consistent exposure metering in the real world will remain a matter of human skill, experience and intuition, not high technology."

I hope that you won't be disappointed if I don't talk more about equipment. There are many good books on the different cameras, and I trust you have read and reread your camera manual several times.

I believe in simplicity when it comes to equipment. Commit yourself to one brand or

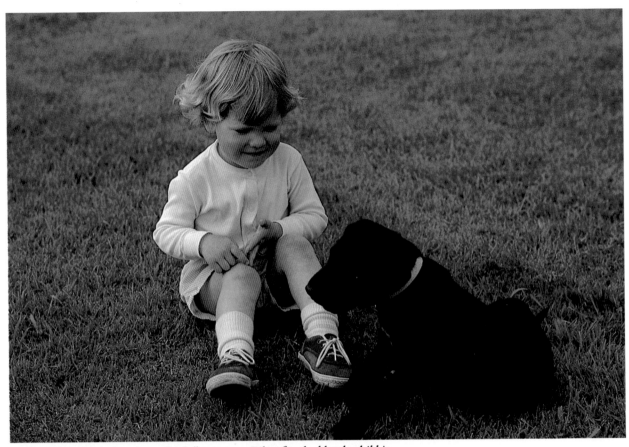

In some situations, there is no "right" exposure. What fits the blonde child is not correct for the black dog, and no compromise would work.

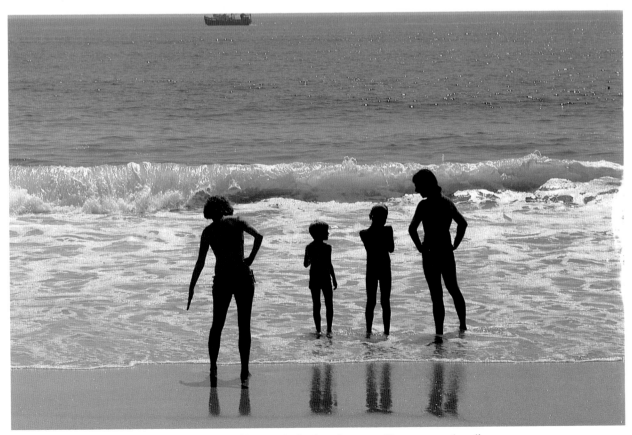

In this photo, exposing the ocean properly and letting the bathers become silhouettes work well.

design of camera, for which all lenses focus in the same direction and are completely interchangeable and all bodies wind and load in the same manner. I haven't regretted sticking for more than 30 years with Minoltas. I have come to handle them as semiautomatically as I drive my car or use a typewriter.

As for accessories, I am unable to combine the use of a tripod with the way I like to move about. I carry filters and sunshades, and that's about all. I put my extra film into a pouch on a belt and add a good felt-tipped pen so that I can write on film ends if I need to. When I have to carry a great deal of film, I keep it in a well-insulated bag (the type usually sold as a food or picnic bag in most five-and-ten stores).

I also recommend separating your equipment evenly into two bags, so that one shoulder does not have to do all the carrying, which can result in progressive injury to your spine. (Check with your doctor; you will learn how important this is for your health.)

In the next few pages, I mention some technical problems that have come up time after time in my own work. They will also be discussed in more detail later. Let's think of some nontechnical problems here, such as:

Composition. I am not referring to aesthetic rules and values because none exist. (Who would have believed even a few years ago that chopped-off heads and random, confusing elements would be hailed in major museums?) But if you often regret that you include unnecessary details, you should learn to "crop" on the film before taking the picture.

Approach. If all your photographs look alike and seem boring, you should try a new approach. Do you immediately instruct your subjects where and how to sit or stand and how to smile? Why not trust chance and your subjects' temperaments? Of course, you will have to put more physical energy into following a lively child rather than instructing him or her to sit on a chair and smile.

Even planned pictures don't have to be boring. Without giving direct orders, you can set the scene and guide the conversation so that you can catch what you are after. Obviously, there are times when it is important that you "produce" a certain picture, but such a shot needn't be the result of strict posing. Try recording a birthday or picnic *without* directing anyone. You will be surprised how much more interesting your photographs will become. You may even have fun discovering the real world of children.

From the realistic to the arranged, you can handle your subject in many ways. Your choice depends on what your aim or assignment is. If you are working on a documentary about children living in slums, you will be deceiving your audience if you try to hide ugly surroundings. For example, you should show a peeling wall if it is part of a child's environment; you should not show it if the wall is peeling because of a temporary mishap and presents a distorted picture of the child's surroundings. But if you are working for a private client or doing an advertisement, you will be considered sloppy if you *don't* try to hide what is ugly or inconsistent.

There are more ways to have the proper background for your photos than by moving into another room. You can, for example, learn to control your background by limiting your depth of field or by finding another angle from which to shoot. Move the camera to the left or right, or higher or lower.

DARE TO MAKE MISTAKES!

Looking at the best photography—whether at exhibits or in books—is sure to develop your taste and widen your horizon. It can also make you feel that everything has already been photographed. Don't believe it! Even if you tried, you couldn't duplicate another person's work. For better or worse, all photographers put their mark on their work, as different and personal as their handwriting or tone of voice.

Learning from books and lectures is admirable, but nothing equals learning by experience. The first rule for producing good photographs is to be there. The second: to become friendly with other photographers and talk shop.

I cannot teach you how to produce perfect pictures every time. I don't even want to. Sure, you can set up two umbrellas, learn the correct exposure, and repeat this setup with perfect technical results every time. But you will then miss dozens of shots happening outside the reach of your umbrellas. I prefer risking marginal exposures, using one light instead of two, and settling for not-so-perfect whites by forgoing umbrellas. (I do not include technical data for most of my pictures because what I do must be obvious. And is it really important whether I shot at 1/100 sec. or 1/250 sec.? Or whether the *f*-stop was *f*/5.6 or *f*/8? Of course, I will mention anything that is special or that needs explanation.)

Using a fast shutter speed is safer than risking blurred action, yet imagine how poetic and lifelike this may be.

If you disobey your automatic camera that begs you to "Use flash! Please use flash!" some parts of your photograph may remain dark. Think, though, how much more effective this may be. Similarly, wide-angle lenses distort your subject. But if the

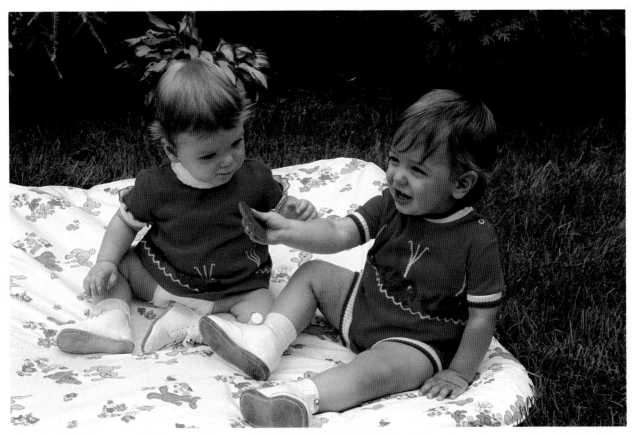

The white blanket was useful for several reasons: to reflect light into the children's faces, to separate two dark colors, and to make the children comfortable.

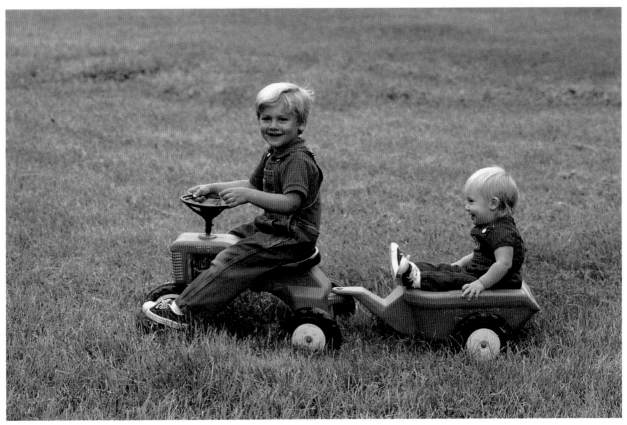

In this shot, no separation of colors was necessary; the red cars and shirts stand out vividly against the green grass.

distortion emphasizes a movement or creates a striking image, using an extra-wide lens (such as 28mm) occasionally can be exciting.

To put it simply, *dare to make mistakes*! It is hard to think of any rule in photography that cannot and should not be broken.

Finally, I hope that studying my photographs—which a critic once called "deceptively simple"—will be useful for your work.

ON BEING A PRO
When I call you a pro, I don't necessarily mean that you are making a great deal of money, or even that you are always taking pictures. You may have accumulated enough knowledge about photography and have produced so much good work that you deserve to be called a professional. (There is nothing wrong with the word "amateur"—it means that you love your work. I hope that you will never stop loving photography.) Let's suppose, though, that you are a full-time photographer. You may take pictures of children in your studio or living room, one after the other, or you may be out there trying to land another advertising account. Is this the kind of life that will help or even permit you to become an excellent photographer?

Doing so won't be easy unless you decide to set aside some time to shoot for yourself, to follow up on an intriguing or beautiful child you have met as a customer or on the bus. A tired mind will not produce fresh ideas for picture stories, and a tired body will not bother to try another way of lighting a picture. An important rule: don't get too tired. You may not have even noticed that you are tired, which can feel like being bored. Of course, the two can be related. If you have only enough energy to keep repeating your usual pictures, you will get bored. But if you do interesting, well-paced work, you won't get tired.

Surprise yourself! Change your lenses, try new angles, use more closeups, and get that new zoom lens out from the bottom of your camera bag where it has been hiding for many months.

Surprise your subjects! Instead of being a worried, preoccupied photographer, be a witty, carefree person, one who is a pleasure to be with. So what if the flash wasn't connected when you started to shoot or if for a while you were doing completely unplanned work.

I suppose this varies somewhat with every photographer, but, in fact, you will spend much less time than you might think actually taking pictures—and much more on getting jobs or clients; talking on the phone; working in the darkroom; and doing your filing, numbering, and general office work.

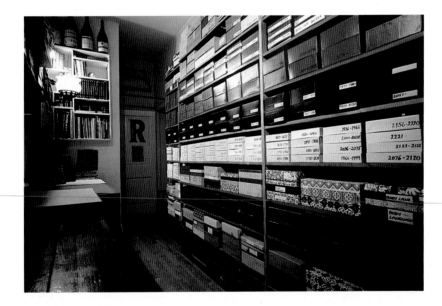

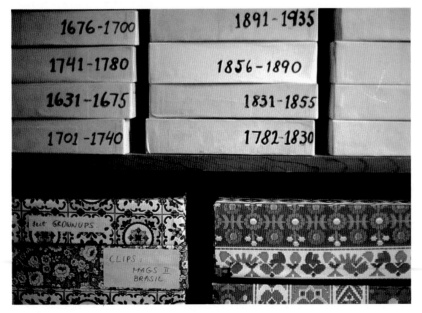

Keeping my files in order by assignment and stock subject is a must; keeping them color-coordinated is a hobby.

Believe me: unless you have trained a full-time person to know your pictures as well as you do and pay him or her accordingly, you must do all the tasks I have mentioned.

As a reward, you will get to know your own work. You can then not only learn from your mistakes and gauge your progress, but also build up a stock file, or write and illustrate articles, and put together a collection of photographs for a book—all of which I have done during my career as a photographer.

Now if only someone would make it easier to handle original color transparency files, I would have no complaints. What are your current choices? To send out original transparencies, trusting that people will handle them carefully and not lose them, or to have copies made? Unfortunately, these are rarely satisfactory, and most clients say, "We want to use your work. But send us the original right away." (I have also tried making my own copies. What a job! And they are no better than what a good lab can do.)

When you have done 2,474 jobs (my total as of yesterday!), you must have a way of quickly finding each and every negative, transparency, contact print, and enlargement. Luckily, I became interested in working out a simple system early, and it has never failed me. Let me explain it.

Each job gets a number, starting with "1"; it may consist of a single roll of a portrait or of 100 rolls of a child growing up. Suppose that you have just completed job number 225. This is what you will write on a simple list: 255 July '86 Maria Parson and family, incl. new puppy. The number goes on all black-and-white negatives, contact prints, and prints as well as the transparencies filed in sheets, each of which contains 20 shots. Parts of a job are not filed together; each goes into

PHOTOGRAPHER
37 EAST 63 ST.
NEW YORK, NY 10021

Photo Release

For valuable consideration and the sum of $ _____,

I hereby give my permission to _____

to use photo No. _____, taken by Suzanne Szasz of me and/or my

child/children named:

_____

for the following purpose: _____

_____

No names will be mentioned.

Signed: _____
                            parent

Address: _____

_____

Date: _____

Witnessed by: _____

PLEASE FILL OUT MARKED PARTS, THEN SIGN AND RETURN BOTH COPIES!

its own box or file drawer, in numerical order. The transparency numbering will look like this: 255 1–4, which means roll 1, frame 4.

My system requires one more item: a Rolodex file with the subject's name and address and the all-important job number (here, 255) marked in red. So, if you remember the name "Parson," you will find the number right away. In less than three minutes, everything connected with job number 255 can be on your desk. If you forget the name "Parson," you have to go by the year the pictures were taken. Because each page of the list is marked with the corresponding year, going

through two or three years of photos won't take very long either.

As you can see from the pictures of my files, I help myself by covering my Kodak paper boxes with adhesive paper of various colors and designs, each with a different meaning. For example, red boxes contain color transparencies; green, paper prints; white, contact prints; and flowery design, clippings.

I store all of these boxes on shelves in a room that is automatically air-conditioned for

Tip: Try to sell a once-a-year photography contract to parents.

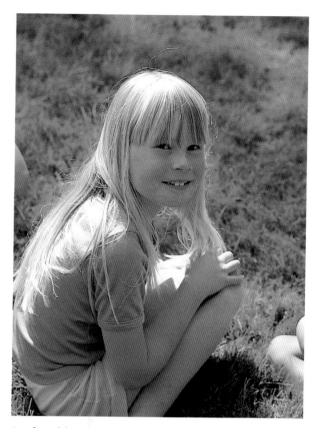

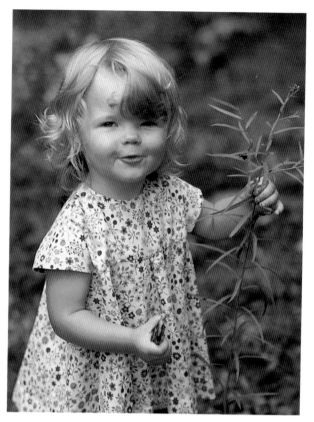

My friends' children and grandchildren make valuable amateur models.

When I see that children enjoy being photographed, I shoot them again and again.

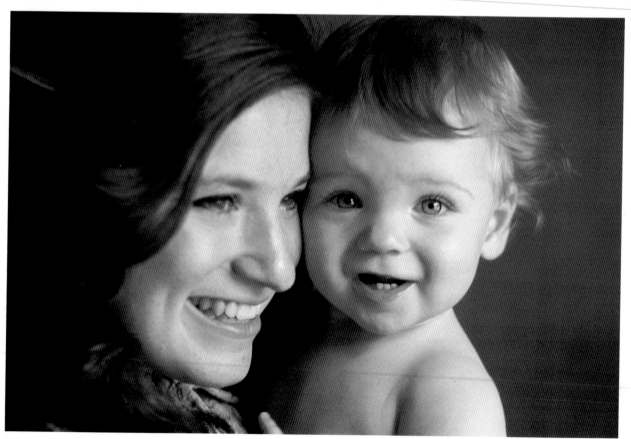

Whatever my main aim or assignment, I always watch for the warm, unplanned scene.

two hours in the middle of each day. Unless I am working in there, I draw the curtains to guard against the light. These conditions should extend the life of my work.

Order and beauty seem to make office work easier for me. My file folders sport different colors and have big pockets. I keep copies of bills sent out in a red folder, copies of correspondence in a gray one. When I receive paid bills from customers, I place the bills in a blue folder; I can then work on putting them into a permanent file whenever I find some "spare" time. I do the same for prints that are returned to me: I put them into an 8 × 10 or an 11 × 14 large box marked "To File." Once a month or so, I file them in numerical order. (I don't want to overwhelm you, but I also have a folder marked "Idea File" and another labelled "To Enlarge for Portfolio.")

Now to an even more important item: releases, or "How to avoid trouble with the people you photograph." Suppose I meet a mother with a beautiful baby in the local supermarket, and we agree that I will come to her home and take some pictures. What next? I don't have the gall to present this unsuspecting mother with one of those airtight, "lawyer-invented" model releases. We agreed that I will submit these pictures to magazines, textbooks, or other noncontroversial outlets and that I will ask her for a release when necessary. At that time, I write my own simple release (see sample), pay her a small model fee, and try to get her a clipping if at all possible. I will then have made a friend. I often locate these subjects years after having taken the pictures. If I include them in a book of my own, I send them a copy of the book—not cheap, but fair. Yes, that is the important word: *fair*. I consider taking pictures

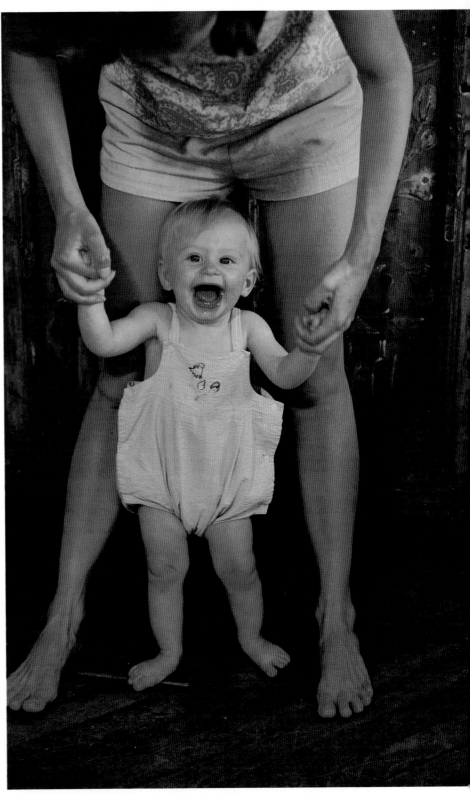

Whenever I see a child who is learning to walk, I take as many shots as I can. I already had this photograph of Christie in my files when an ad agency requested this exact situation.

Tip: When selling stock shots for advertising, charge as much as for an assignment. You save the client time and expense by having the needed shot ready.

15

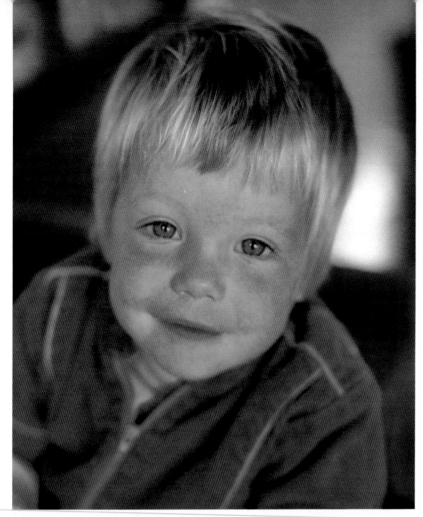

The dream of all private customers: an angelic smile on the face of their little imp.

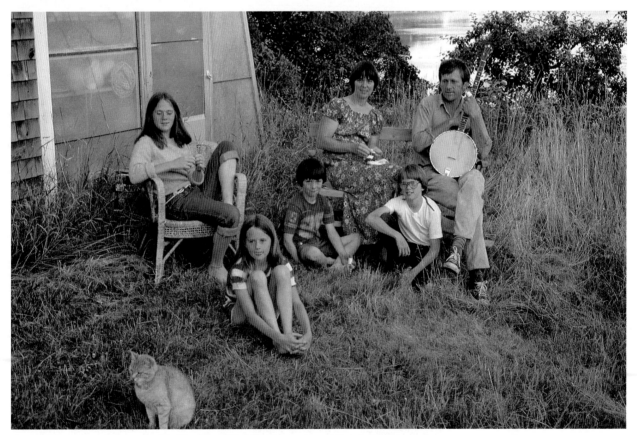

A posed but relaxed shot of a family whose life I had been chronicling in Maine. Their attention was focused on their cat instead of me.

a joint venture and have never regretted the amount of effort and money that goes into my method.

ONE IMPORTANT NOTE: I do want to emphasize, however, that this is simply my own personal method. I strongly suggest that, at the very least, you obtain a copy of the American Society of Magazine Photographers (ASMP) guidelines for releases. (Contact ASMP at 205 Lexington Ave., New York, NY 10016.)

THE HELP YOU NEED
Some photographers may need to supplement their income either by printing for others or by taking part-time jobs that leave them enough time and energy for their own work. I know of photographers who worked as part-time book editors, teachers' helpers, camera store salespeople, writers, and even tennis instructors while on their way to becoming full-time photographers.

Once I was established, and although I consider myself a one-person operation, at different times in my career I had the help of several people and organizations. When most of my work was black-and-white, I needed a printer. Since I didn't have enough work for a full-time helper, I solved the problem by offering the use of my darkroom to a person who would print for me once or twice a week. That left making exhibition prints and enlargements for my own books to me, which is the way I like it.

Tip: Instead of suggesting ideas and outlines, try to approach a magazine editor with a finished story. This can be a simple set of pictures, but it should have a beginning, a middle, and an end; it should also be suitable for that particular publication.

In the beginning, I was surprised to find that reps wanted to work with photographers who were already making respectable sums of money. "We can more than double your money," they promised. I opted for visiting art directors and editors on my own and have never been sorry. I think it was time well spent on learning their opinions and requirements. I do, however, know of other photographers whose careers blossomed after a rep had assisted in developing the direction of their work.

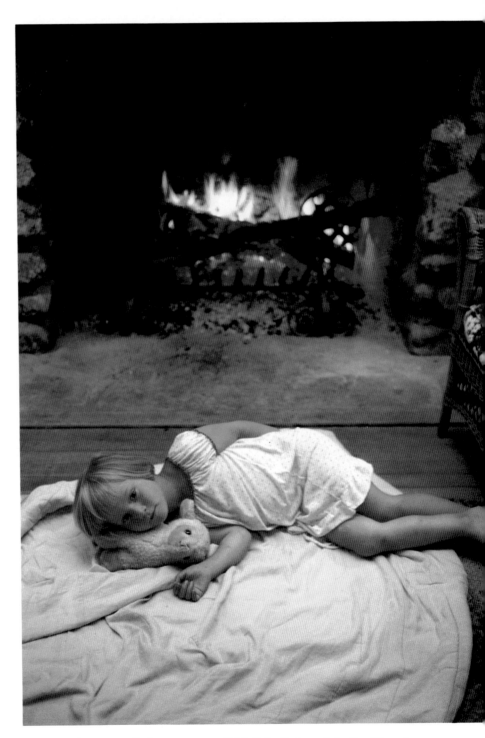

A rare combination of light sources: available light, flash, and the fire. The colors may not be faithful, but the atmosphere is.

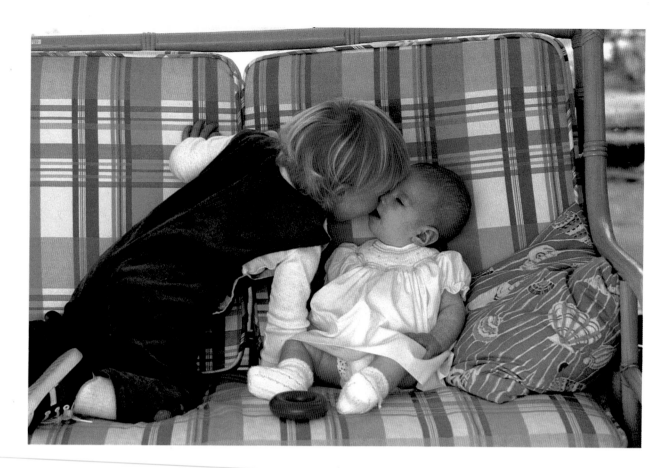

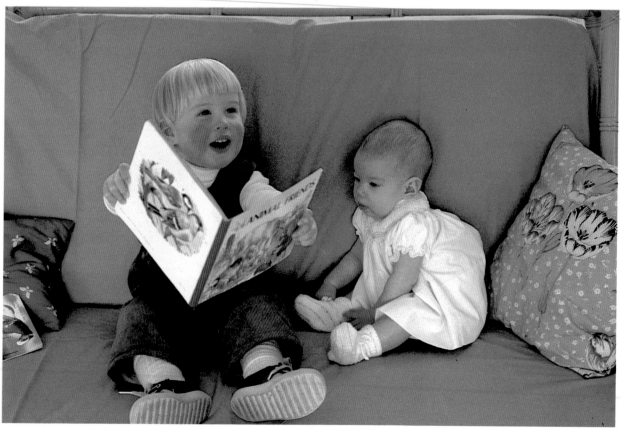

In the case of the two children on the couch, the loud pattern kept bothering me: I could barely find the children's faces because there were so many lines. I then draped a plain sheet over the couch. When the children returned, I found the background much more pleasing.

About 15 years ago, I met the people who comprise the Photo Researchers agency. I like and respect them, and we have never had arguments about money, even when we happened to contribute to the same book. (Editors or researchers came and bought from my files; they also bought work of mine that was in the agency's files.)

It is not the agency's fault that I am having problems with surrendering the originals of my best color work to its files, and clients dislike dupes. I do try to take more than one original of the same situation—but children rarely hold still (unlike landscapes or posed subjects).

Throughout my career, I have valued the help that ASMP has given me. Not only is it instructive to listen to the best people in our field explain some aspects of their work, it is enjoyable to meet your colleagues on a regular basis. And it is important to feel that you are not alone when you fight for more money and all rights to your pictures.

Another group, American Picture Professionals (APP), also holds monthly meetings where you can meet not only photographers, but also others working in the publishing field.

A few years ago, some of us founded Professional Women Photographers (PWP) in order to share our knowledge and experience with women just starting out. At some of the gatherings of this group, I was able to meet women whose names and work had long been familiar to me.

Finally, I would like to mention two books that can be of great help. *Selling Your Photography* (New York: St. Martin's Press, 1986) deals with all the various aspects of the business side of photography. Its authors are Arie Kopelman and Ted Crawford. The other book, *Professional Business Practices in Photography* (New York: ASMP, 1986), is an excellent compilation of such matters as sample agreements, release forms, and ways of settling disputes.

Tip: Be sure that your photographs include both sexes, all ages, and a good mix of races if you want to sell to textbook publishers.

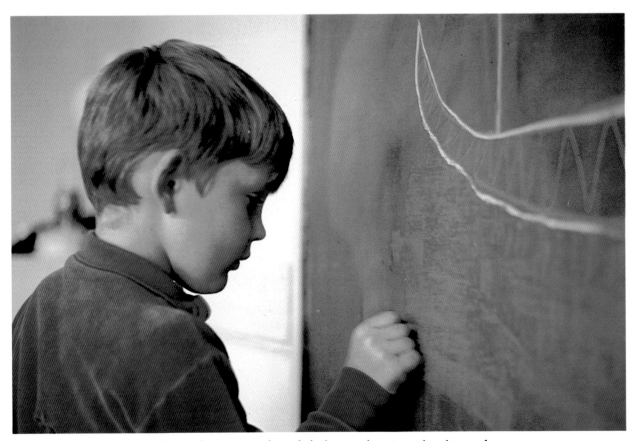

Textbook publishers often ask for stock pictures and are glad when you have just what they need.

TECHNICAL BASICS

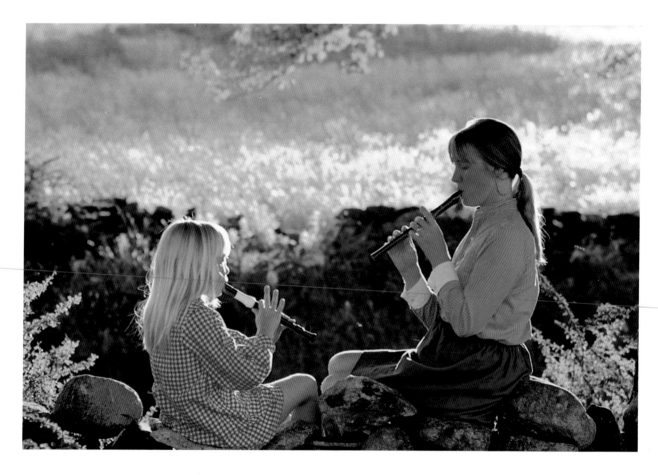

I have been looking in vain for an example of a color picture taken with the sun behind me. I didn't think I would have to shoot one especially for this book: all of you have seen them already. People are likely to squint or wear dark glasses; the colors lack subtlety. With very few exceptions, all such photographs look amateurish to me. That's why I have grown so accustomed to shooting against the sun. This is not easy on my eyes, but it is comfortable for the people I photograph.

Sunlight looks magical when it hits the outline of a figure or a child's blond head. But sunlight can also fool you as well as automatic cameras since only a small part of the picture is touched by the sunlight. As a result, you need to increase the exposure so that everything in the shade is also properly lit.

I took this photograph of a mother and daughter playing their recorders for a Creative Playthings Brochure. I chose the spot for the picture carefully. I knew that I would not need any fill-in as there was another patch of well-lit grass behind me, which helped to lighten the figures. I opened up one stop, then two stops more than the overall metering indicated. I finished the roll in this manner while enjoying the duets my subjects played.

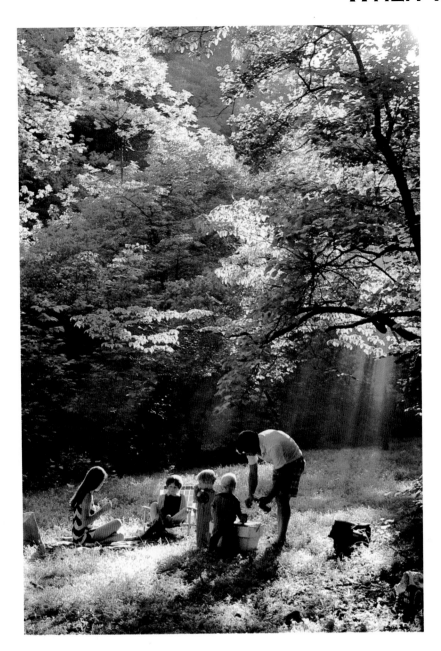

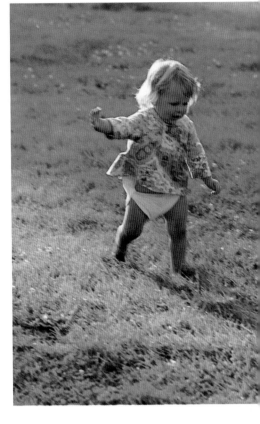

Sunlight can come from the front, back or side; its effect also depends on the angle of the sun. Each season changes the angle, as does the time of day. Photographs taken in the morning have a cool, bluish look; late in the afternoon, you notice a warm tone. This is determined by the angle at which sunlight passes through the different layers of the atmosphere. As the sun goes down, its rays can produce magic.

A little clearing in the woods of Maryland, a picnicking family, and beautiful backlit trees are the ingredients that make this picture one of my favorites. I tend to prefer photographs of mine that "just happened." This is not because I don't like to work, but because "accidental" photographs somehow feel more authentic.

I watched this little girl as she happily practiced her newly acquired skill of walk-

ing. This is the best of the shots I caught, backlit by the sun and frontlit by the sunny patch of lawn in the foreground. (I don't know how this picture escaped having an overall green tinge.)

Of course, *I had to be there.* That is the one most indispensable element of any picture. You have to invest your time, really enjoy working with people, be there from start to finish, and take advantage of any lucky break.

FILLING IN AGAINST THE SUN

When you work near sand, light pavement, or a sunlit wall, you can take advantage of the way each lightens the shaded parts of the picture. In this photograph, practically every blade of grass shimmers and the two little girls stand out against the greenery as if lit by special spotlights. No fill-in was necessary; the sand at the children's feet provides that. But you cannot always depend on finding foregrounds or natural reflectors that eliminate the need for artificial fill-ins. As a result, you should be prepared with a good small electronic flash, which can be used either directly or bounced off a white card.

How much fill-in you need depends on the strength of the sunlight, the distance between you and your subject, and the power of your electronic flash unit. When you shoot directly, you can figure out your f-stops using tables and your instruction booklet.

I suggest that you make your own tests, too. Start by taking an overall meter reading of a backlit subject and add fill without making any adjustment in the exposure. Then advance a few feet and shoot again. Next, return to your original spot and after stepping back a few feet, shoot again. Now bracket by both opening and closing your lens one f-stop each time. It not only sounds complicated, it is. Therefore, keep a completely accurate record of all your shots: film type, speed, f-stop, distance from subject, and camera model. Be sure to ask your film lab to give you back your developed roll uncut; then you can keep comparing each shot to the corresponding data on your record.

After you choose the best five or six shots, have them framed at the lab, and then record all information on the cardboard frame. Here is an example: Kodachrome 64, 1/60 sec. at f/11, from 5 feet away, Minolta 320 electronic flash at full power.

Remember, you must use 1/60 sec.—unless you have one of the new cameras that allow you to synchronize your flash at 1/100 sec. or 1/250 sec. And, yes, even automatic electronic flashes should be tested.

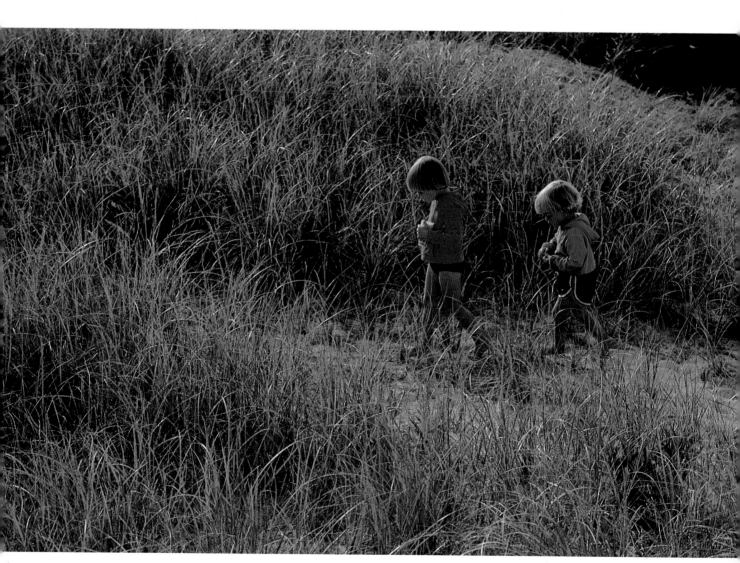

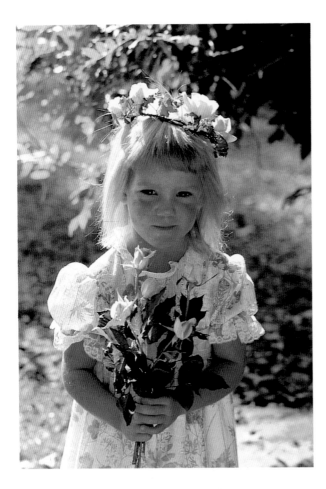

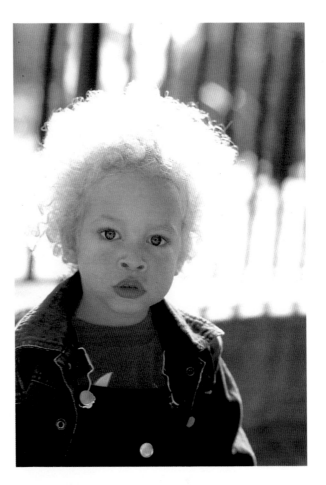

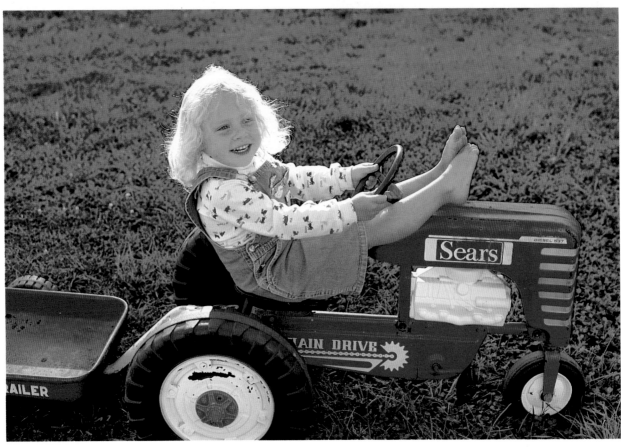

WITHOUT SUN

This is not an easy section for me to write because the subject matter is so simple and natural: avoiding harsh direct lighting, aiming instead for soft, even illumination. I have photographed instinctively this way from the day I started out.

I wonder. Doesn't everyone think that not using cumbersome equipment whenever possible makes sense? Hasn't everyone noticed that the meter reading is nearly identical whether the sun is shining or is hidden behind white clouds? And isn't the world of children especially suited to be portrayed in pastel tones?

If so, do I need to discuss the convenience and beauty of shooting without sunshine? But, more than that, I am urging you to dash out to hunt for wonderful pictures when you notice that the sky is cloudy.

That's exactly what I did when I asked a friend if I could spend some time with her three-year-old daughter. The little girl was in her tree house, playing with her teddy bear. I love the results: two little round heads framed in a larger circle.

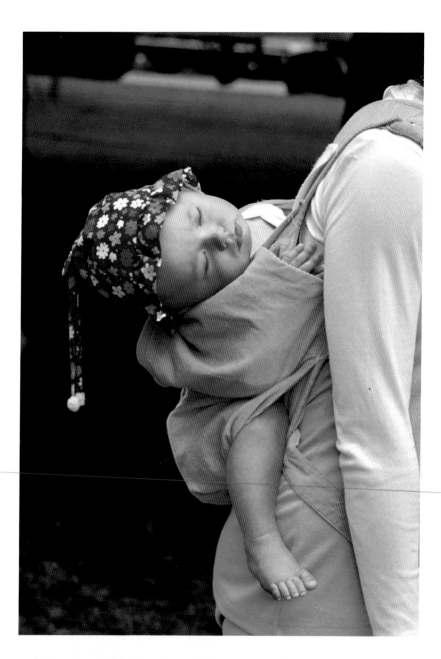

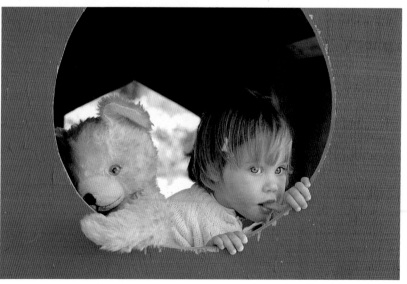

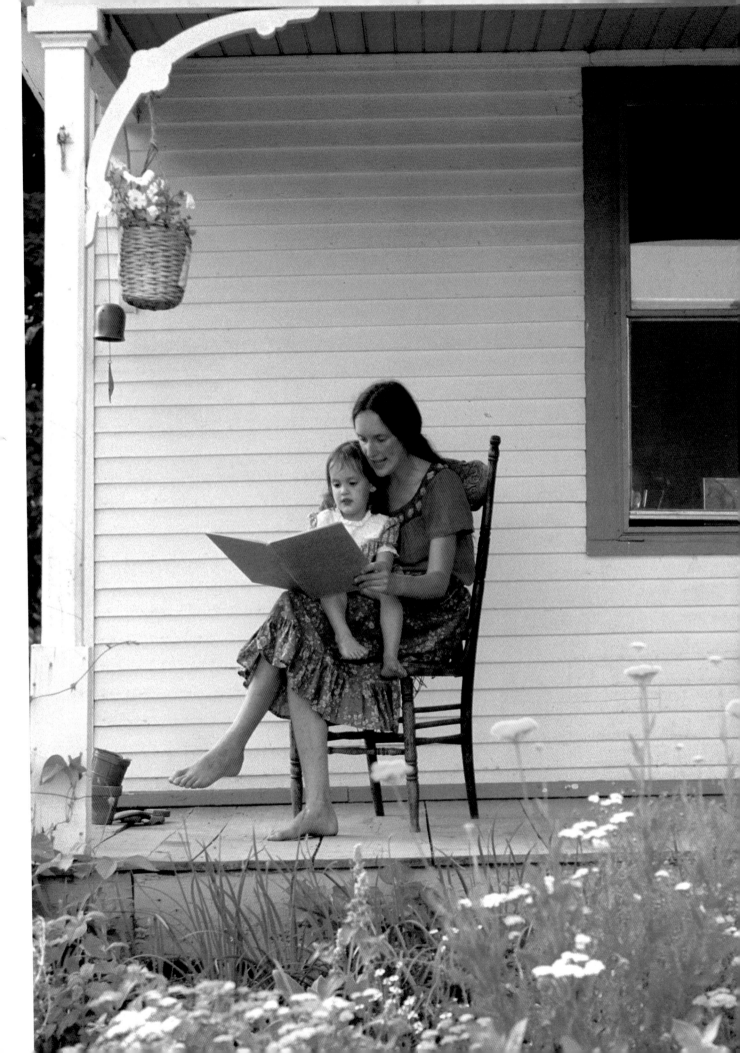

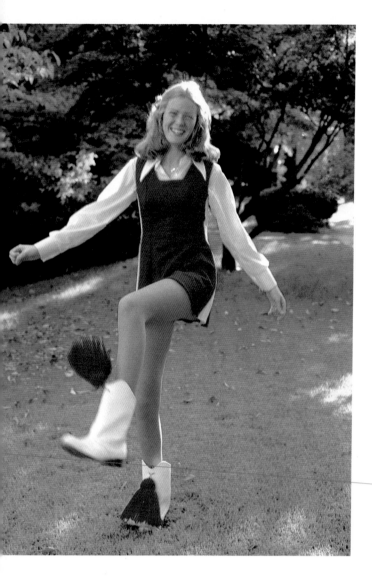

I wouldn't dream of doing a book that did not include the picture on the opposite page: it is one of my favorites. It has already been used in two of my earlier books. This was not an easy picture to take because there were about 100 guests walking to an outdoor wedding. It took a great deal of jockeying on my part to isolate my friend and her young daughter from the crowd.

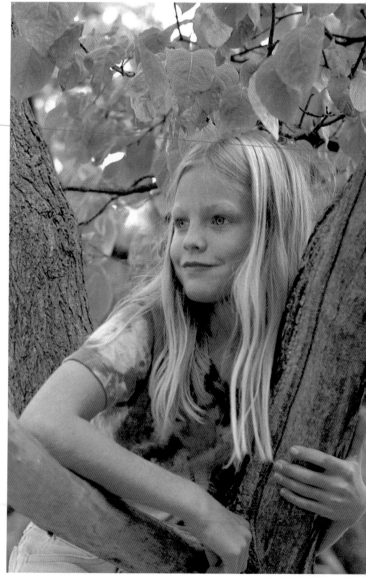

On another day, Sonja, whom I have known since she was a baby, wanted to demonstrate her cheerleading talents to me; I asked her to dance on the shady part of the lawn. In this picture, she moved into one of the small patches of direct sun coming through the trees. When you examine how different the lawn looks where the sun changes its color, you can imagine the unpleasant effect the sun would have had if it had lit Sonja's face.

I like to encourage the children I photograph to ask a friend to come along with us. This way they can talk and play and forget about me and my camera. Sophie was showing her tree climbing ability to a friend when I caught her with a 100mm lens.

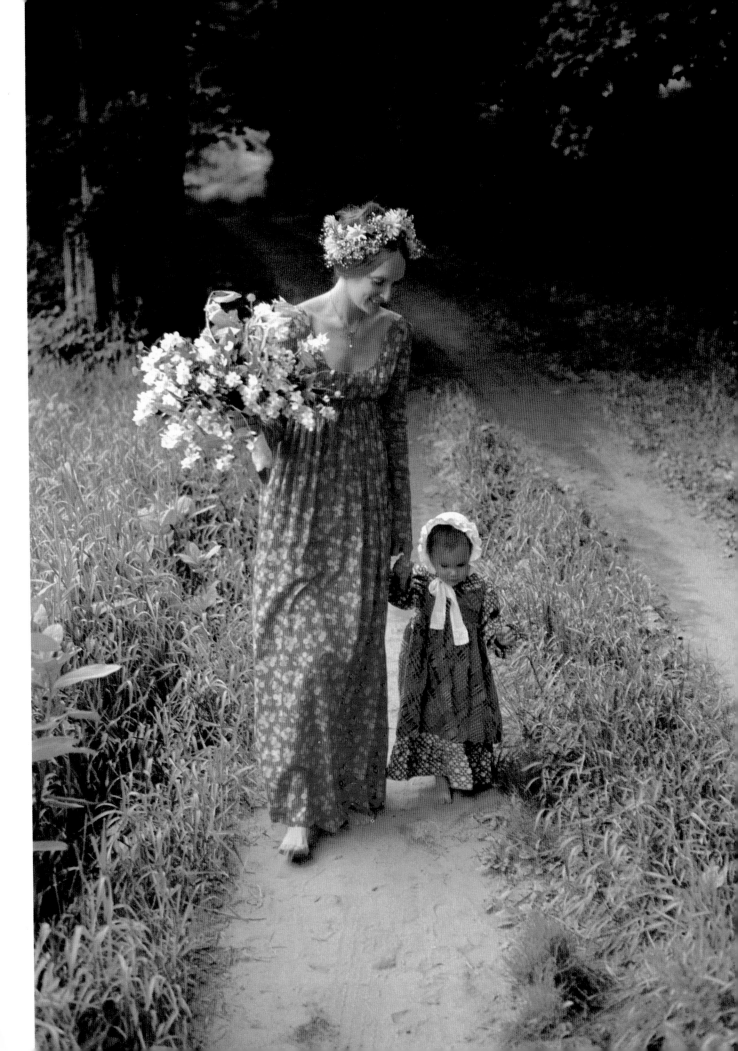

Available Light Indoors

I think that these pictures help to explain the advantages of being ready to shoot at a moment's notice. Whatever the light, the situations are so unexpected and interesting that you simply have to take a chance. Advertising your presence will immediately change and ruin whatever you like about the scene; this rules out using flash unless you are willing to settle for only one shot.

The little girl is emptying her mother's dresser drawer. I am sure she would never have done this had she not been left alone in the bedroom after I took some photographs of her there learning to tie her shoes.

It is important to let life just happen by removing yourself from a scene after a while. When you come back, you will see what the children really felt like doing.

A final point about this shot: I set the 35mm lens at 1/30 sec. at $f/4$, which is not recommended for an action shot, I know; but the result justifies having taken the chance.

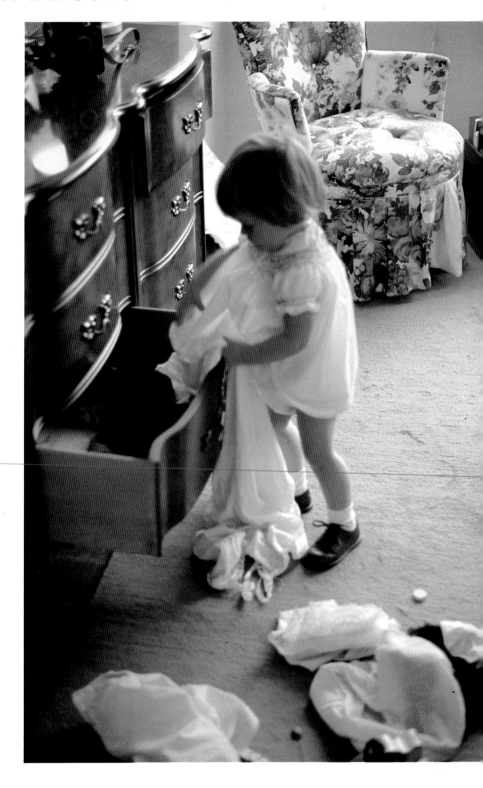

When I walked into this Maine kitchen, I saw that Joshua and his mother were having an important discussion. I had no lighting problems as there were windows on all sides. Knowing I had to draw the line between catching the moment and eavesdropping, I took just two or three shots with an 85mm lens. I then left and let mother and son finish their talk.

It is not unusual to want to see and hear everything. But I believe that children deserve privacy, too, and I can justify my intrusion only by believing that I contribute by recording their emotional lives.

I once left two photographs out of one of my books because my nine-year-old subject, who had been in the bathtub, protested. The boy's mother didn't mind, but we both thought it was important not to embarrass her son.

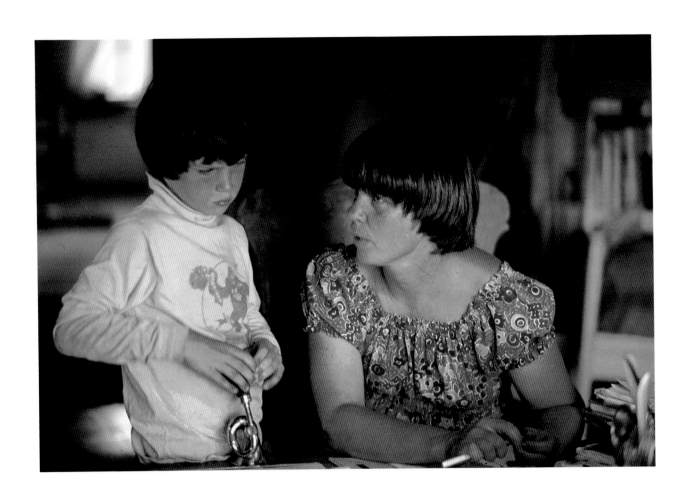

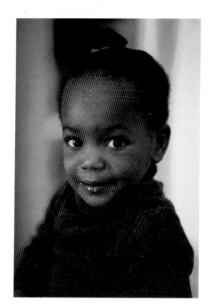

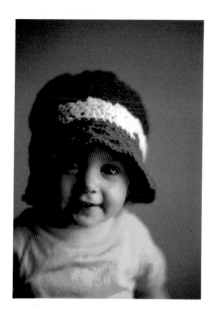

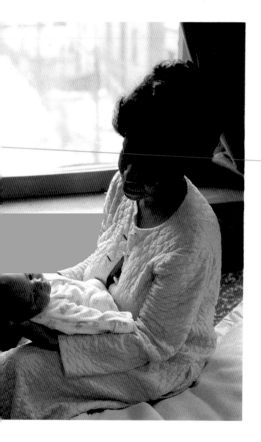

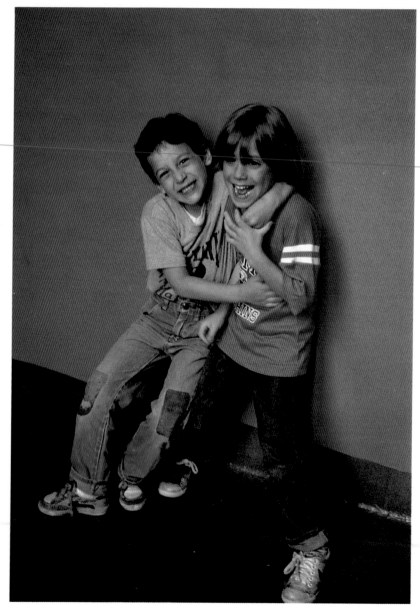

Each picture has its own little story, of course: a new knit hat or a favorite red shirt that the girls are happy to show off, a friendly tussle in a school corridor, a quiet moment as a mother watches her baby fall asleep in her lap, and the difficult time a teenager has trying to write a thank-you note at the kitchen table.

These are all scenes of everyday life that I was able to capture by using available light. I concentrated on what was happening, and allowed life to unfold without my direction. I believe that this approach will help you take really good photographs of children.

To put it simply, I wish I could always work with available light. With it I can fulfill my aims as a photographer. I want people to share what I see when a four-day-old infant smiles back at her mother. I also want people to understand that their children can feel pain and joy and express a range of emotions so fleetingly that sometimes everyone is surprised when the camera catches them.

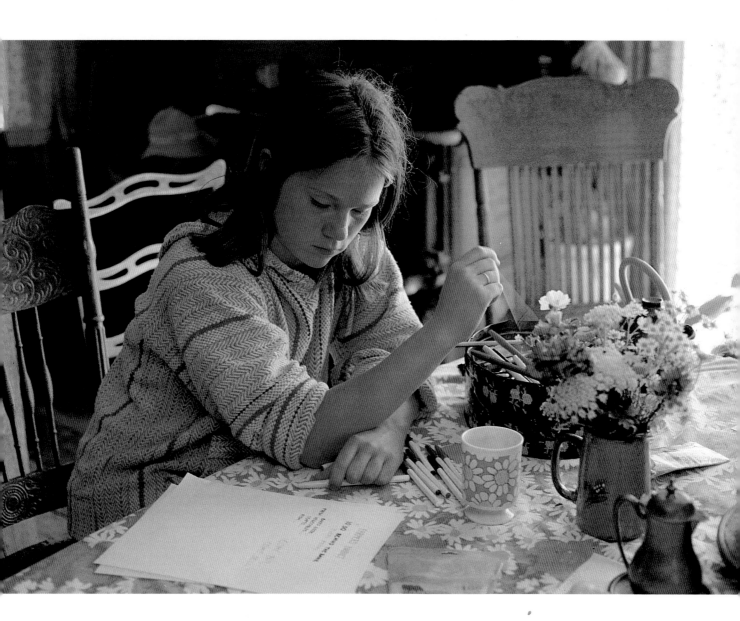

Direct Flash

It would be pretentious on my part to suggest that I know all the ins and outs of direct-flash photography. I shied away from it when I started, and I only use this method of lighting pictures when nothing else will work. In most large halls, such as school gyms, it would be hard to think of any other way to take pictures in the evening.

I admit that there are many advantages to direct-flash photography. Even a small flash unit produces good pictures when used direct; it stops fast action. And with automatic units you don't even have to worry about the exposure.

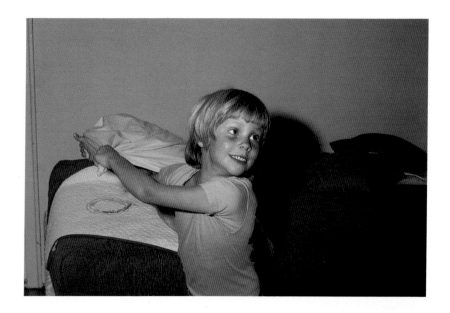

But once you start using an electronic flash, you will find it difficult if not impossible to keep your subjects from noticing what you're doing. Also, the closer your subjects are to the background, the more noticeable the shadows will be. Only experience will teach you how to minimize them.

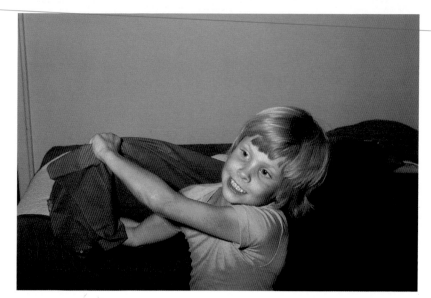

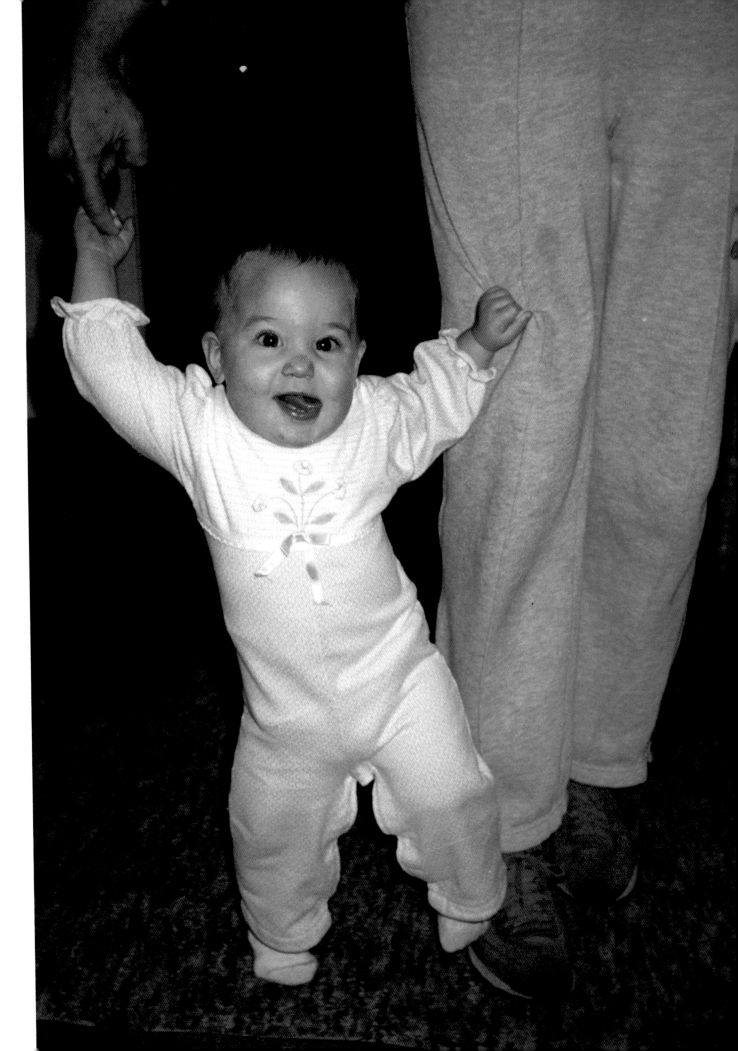

DIRECT FLASH

As do all other methods, direct-flash photography has its applications. This can be seen in the work of both Jill Freedman and Weegee. Maybe *you* will utilize direct flash in children's pictures better than anyone else ever has.

As for technique: read your manual, and then read it again. And remember—whether or not your unit is automatic—make your own tests, as I discussed earlier.

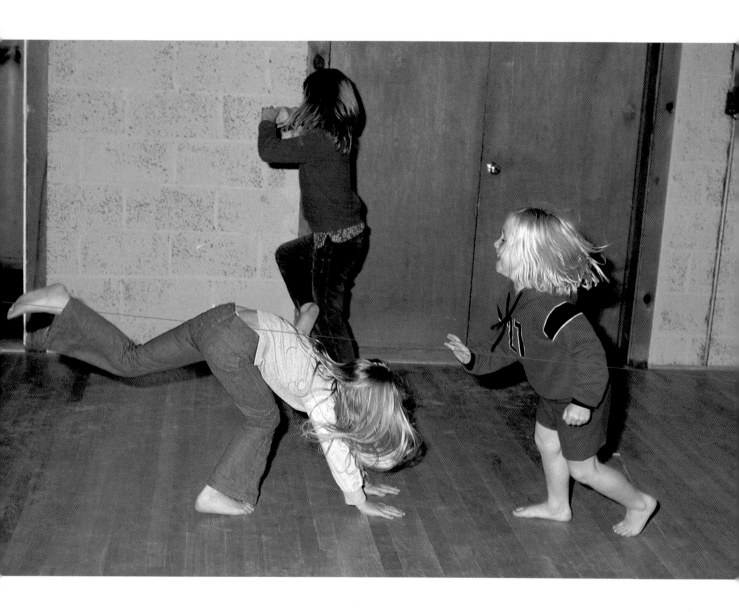

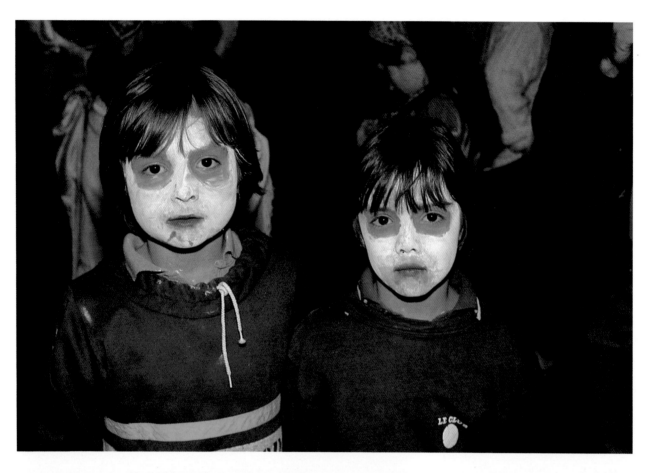

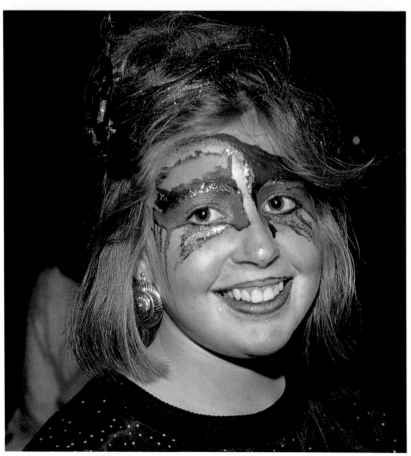

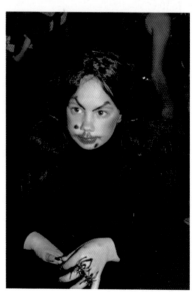

BOUNCE FLASH

Hurray for small but powerful electronic flash units that swivel on a camera or light-stand and bounce light off ceilings or walls. After some trial and error, most of your pictures will look as if they were illuminated by available light.

But I must warn you: it is very hard to predict exactly how the height of the ceiling or another reflecting surface will affect the colors in your photograph. Only lengthy experience will give you the know-how to shoot within two stops of the correct exposure. After a while, you will walk into a room, notice the color of the walls, look up, estimate the height of the ceiling, and think, "That's an $f/4$ ceiling."

Today, automatic flash units let you take a test shot, and if you guess correctly, a little green (or red) "OK" light goes on for a few seconds.

If you have to shoot in a room with a ceiling that is very high and/or dark, you can save your photos by mounting your electronic flash on the stem of a white umbrella. (I must admit that I use this setup only when I have an assistant who carries my gear and makes sure no child bumps into the light-stand to which the umbrella is attached.) Now you won't have to guess and take test shots: you will know what exposure your particular flash and umbrella require.

This is a wonderful way to work when taking posed shots—but attention-getting and not very mobile. Getting really candid shots is hard when your camera is connected to a flash that is mounted on a lightstand . . . on top of which sits an umbrella . . . all steadied by an assistant. . . .

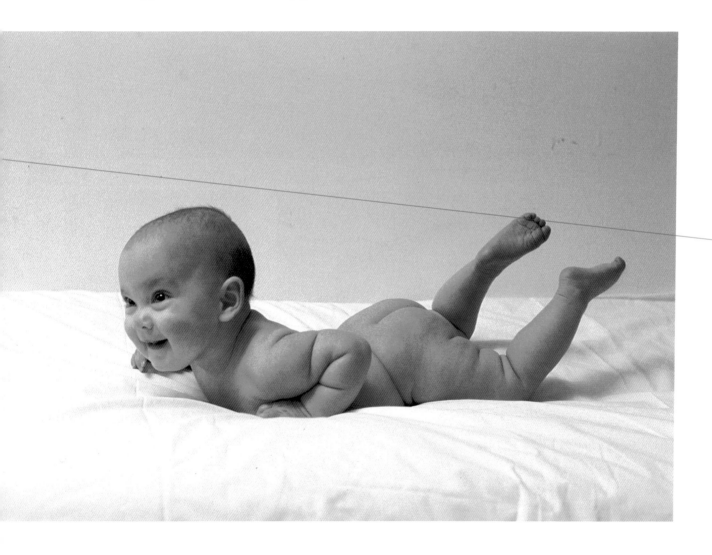

For this mother-child picture, using an umbrella was possible because the baby was still; I would not, however, have been able to set up in time to catch the little girls in the picture on the right, who were trying to go out the door.

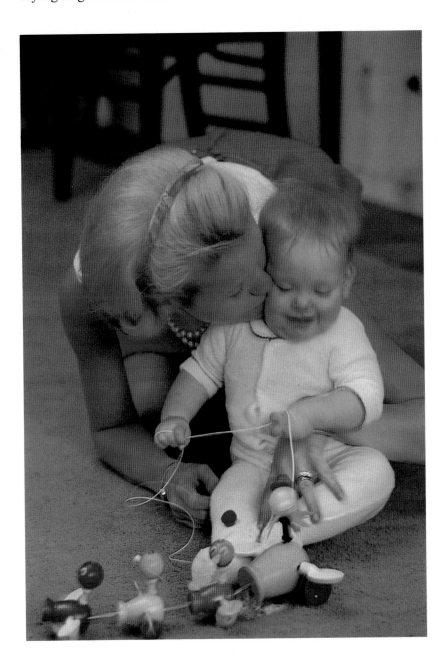

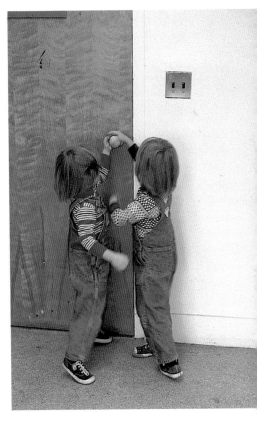

Now, some technical information about bounce flash. It is not easy to deal with such complex electronic wonders as the automatic flash unit when you want to fill in the shaded areas. I prefer to use my electronic flash on the manual setting, which allows me better control of the fill-in.

As usual, I make several tests, writing down exactly what I do (later I make sure that the lab returns my roll uncut). First I change my output control from full to ½, then to ¼. Next, I vary the distance from subject to electronic flash and shoot some tests at different *f*-stops. Then I weaken the fill-in by resetting the flash's film speed indicator to a higher ISO. And, finally, there is the old-fashioned method of putting a diffuser on the flash head, all in manual mode.

You can also try one of the newest (and simplest) methods: placing a plain white 4 × 6 card behind your flash. If you are handy, add some Velcro to both the flash and the card so you can put on and take off the card easily. A couple of rubber bands can also do the job. When the flash head is pointed straight up, this card will "direct-bounce" some of the light onto your subject. In the picture at the bottom of the opposite page, you can even see "catch lights" in the child's eyes.

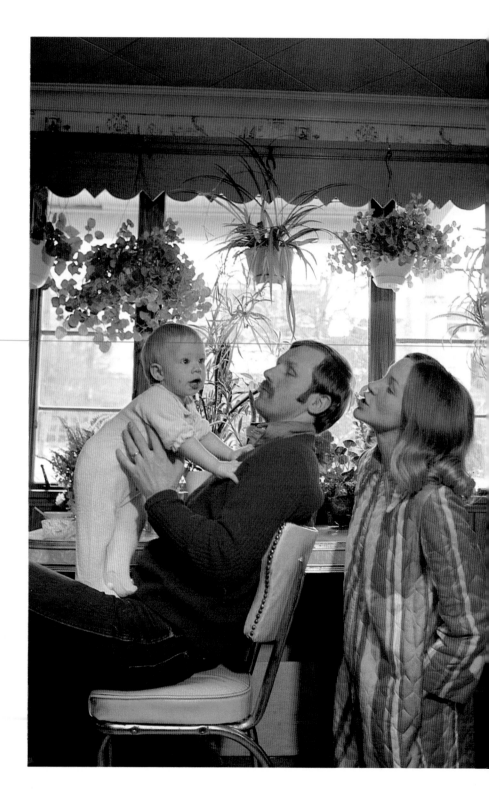

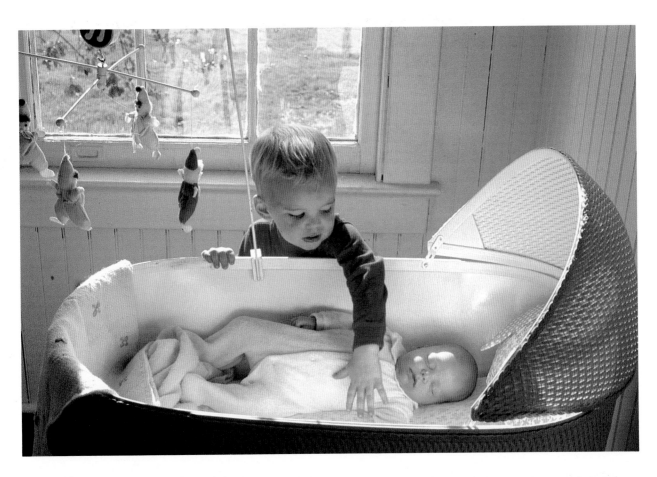

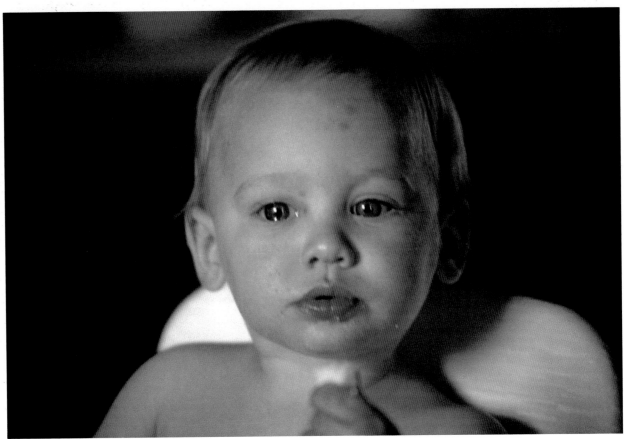

TUNGSTEN LIGHTS

I would not be surprised if many of you have never used tungsten lights and film or even heard much about them. (In this section any reference to floods or reflector floods means tungsten light, designed to be used with tungsten-balanced film.)

When I started out, working in black and white, I usually augmented available light by clamping a photoflood to a bookcase or shelf or by putting one light on a stand. I was then set to shoot anywhere in the room. People's eyes quickly got used to the increased illumination, and I felt that no one knew when I was taking my pictures.

Except in rooms with very dark walls and very high and/or dark ceilings, I was able to bounce my lights off the ceiling or walls. This gave me lighting so natural that I have trouble determining if I had augmented the available light.

When I started to work in color, I discovered that photofloods also came in blue to complement light for daylight-balanced color film. So for a long time I carried the necessary reflectors (blue photofloods don't come in the compact mushroom shape). Then one day I must have accidentally used tungsten photofloods to fill in on daylight film. The resulting pictures were warmer in tone than usual; whites especially tended to be yellowish. But in many cases, the golden light was quite pleasant, particularly when the needed fill-in was not strong. This has remained an option in my shooting ever since.

A third alternative is using tungsten-balanced film with tungsten lights. This is fine for late afternoon or evening or for rooms without windows, as tungsten film registers the daylight coming in from outside as an odd shade of blue.

Tungsten lights are wonderful when you are learning to improve your backgrounds. You can *see* how to adjust your lights in order to eliminate a disturbing element in a background. This will serve you well when you want to use electronic flash (when you cannot see the light you will eventually get).

It is easy to light up a room so that you can take pictures from most angles. All you need to do is to secure two 500-watt reflector floods in opposite corners of the room. If the ceiling is a typical low, white surface, you can bounce the lights off it; if not, use them directly. A word of caution: you *must* be sure that the wires are secured in such a way that the children cannot reach them and possibly hurt themselves.

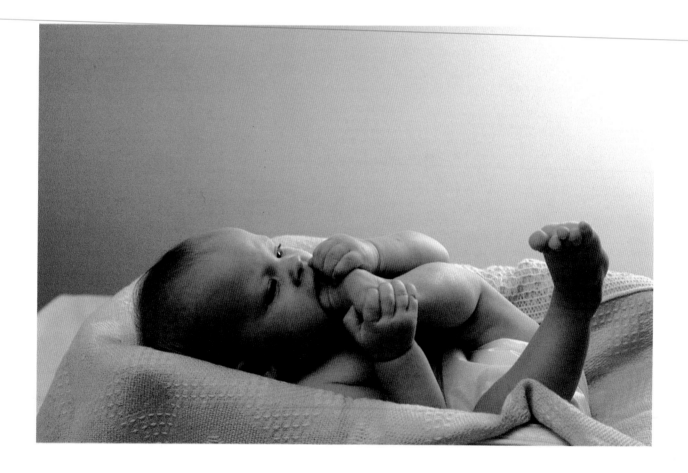

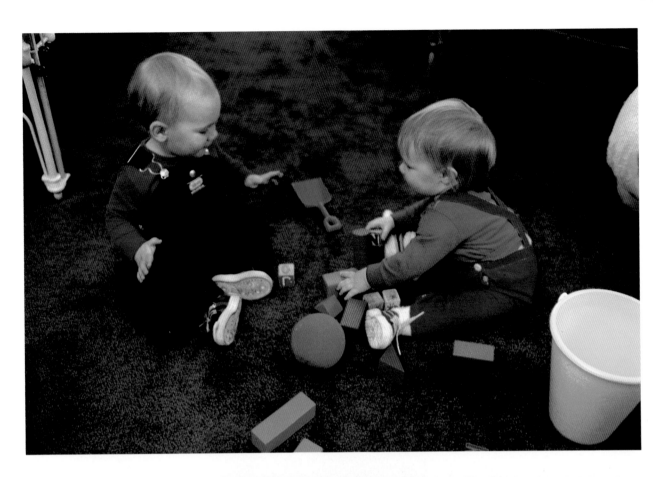

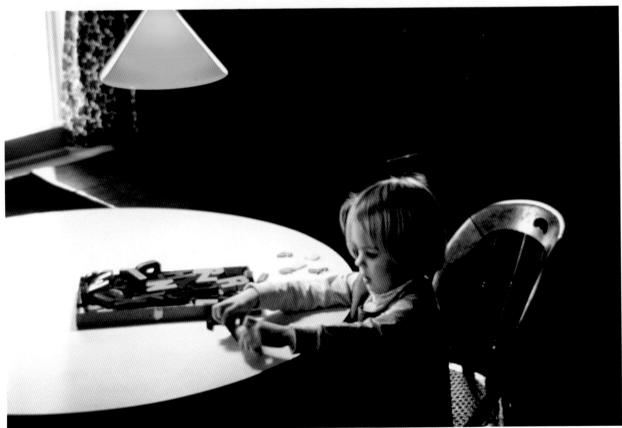

TUNGSTEN LIGHTS

In the picture on the right, some fluorescent light was also present in the classroom.

In the picture below, I had one direct photoflood in the back, another direct light in the front—and the father standing by to make sure that no one got tangled in the wires. Never try such a setup without an assistant or with other children in the room; it is too dangerous. (I have never had an accident with my lights, but I am always very careful.)

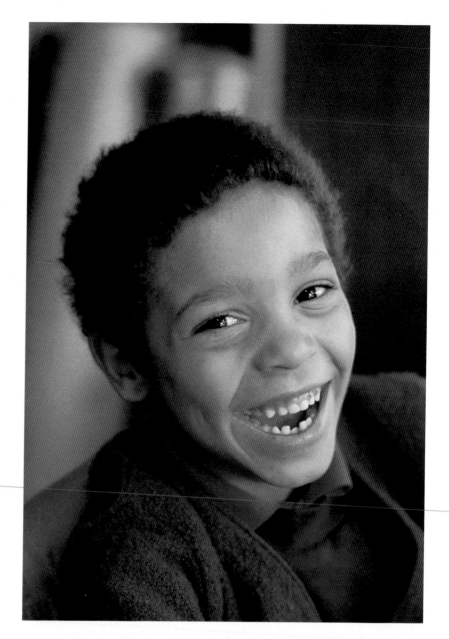

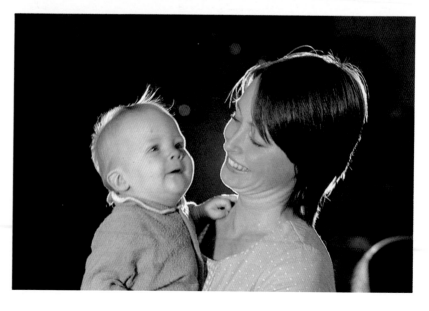

In the photo on this page, the little blonde girl was posed in front of the plain white wall in her room. The wall was illuminated by one direct reflector flood. She sat about four feet from the wall; I stood about six feet from her, with a photoflood slightly to my left, aimed directly at her face. Not many children can be trusted to be patient and tolerate the strong light, but I knew that Fairley was delighted to be photographed for a sweater ad.

Although many children are born models, I tend to discourage mothers who are eager for their children to become professionals. I remind them how hard it is for both of them to go from studio to studio, whether their offspring feel like posing that day or not.

I consider my work to be the recording of every facet of childhood. I appreciate my friendship with many families that allow me to use their children as "models" when I have an assignment for a specific shot, be it of a "baby eating" or a "boy riding hobby-horse." And I don't think that the children are hurt by posing in their own home when they look forward to the toy they are going to get and when the mothers know that they will have a check to put into the children's bank account. Most children also enjoy the attention that accompanies photography. I treat them with my usual patience and appreciate what they contribute to the original idea for the photograph.

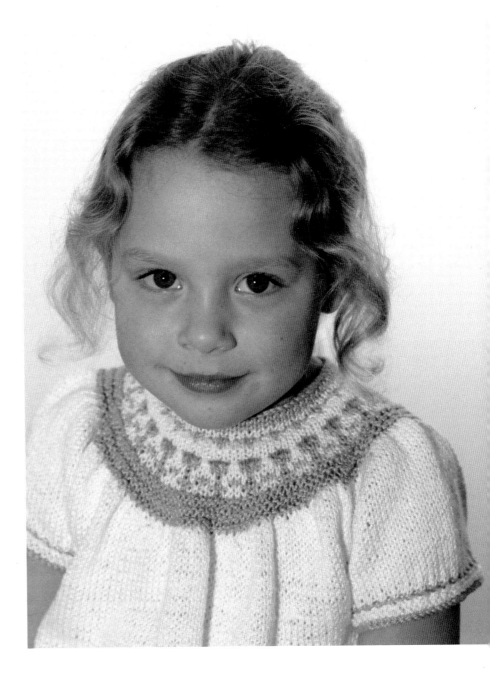

No, the photographs of plants and cats you see on these two pages are not included here by mistake. I think that they can be useful when you want to experiment. The best manual will not tell you any more about depth of field or the effect of lenses with varying focal lengths than will going out and seeing the result in your pictures. As Andreas Feininger advises in one of his books, "If you have to say 'Hold still!'— you better photograph flowers that *do* hold still!"

Well, cats don't hold still, nor do they take kindly to being moved from one chair to another, or even being turned to look to the left or right. And you can't ask them to do so. You just have to catch them when the light is good, when they seem to be in the mood to stay where they are, and when they have gotten used to you. Some cats are afraid of the camera—and so are some children. (After all, you "shoot" them, don't you?)

I believe that a person who can record a cat's life will be able to do the same with children. So, if you are contemplating doing a photo project on your own children, you should practice on a cat in order to become an expert on sensing what your subjects may do next and to observe and photograph them quickly and sensitively. You may even catch a yawn! And then, when you start on your project with your children, they will thank you and your results will be much better.

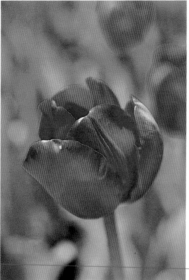 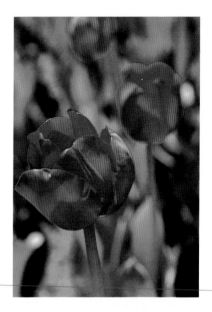

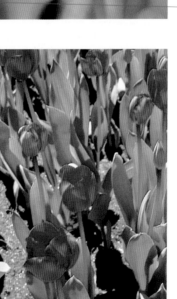 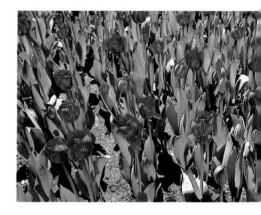

The same tulips taken from the same spot with a 135, 85, 50, and 35mm lens, respectively.

44

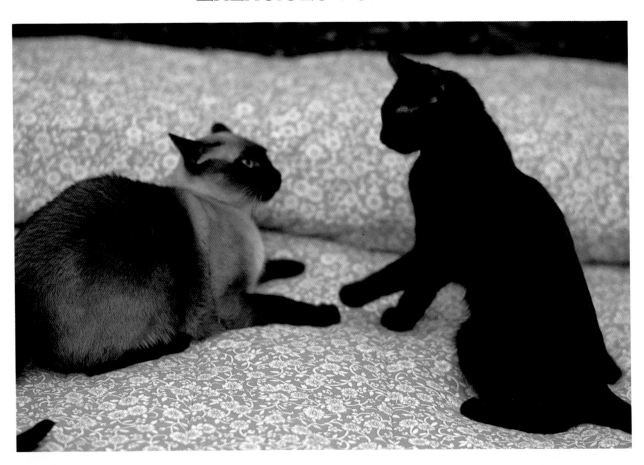

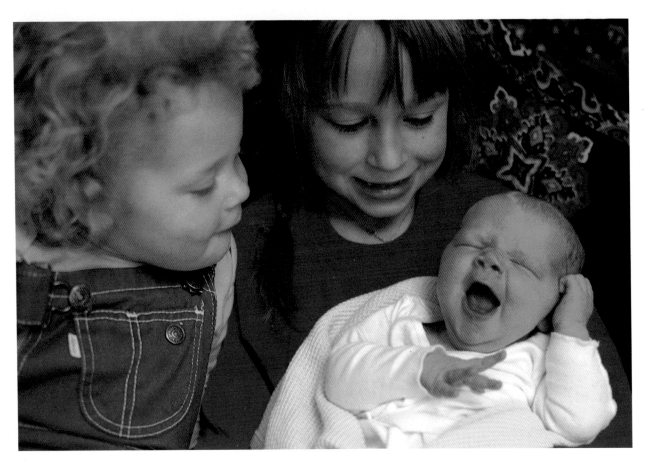

Different Angles

One of the surest ways to add some freshness to your photographs is to vary your angles. Viewing scenes from ground level or from high above produces a pleasant shock.

I am always aware of stairs, balconies, and second-floor windows because they can introduce a new perspective in a familiar scene. There is a fringe benefit: such vantage points also let me photograph without being noticed. As you can see, what might have been an ordinary photo of a child looking in a mirror is dramatized both by the high point of view and the use of a 35mm lens.

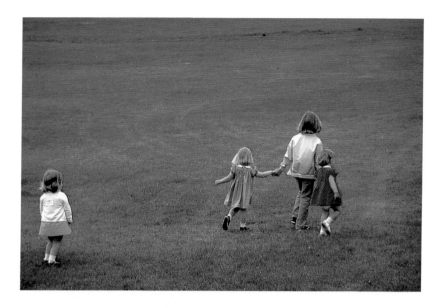

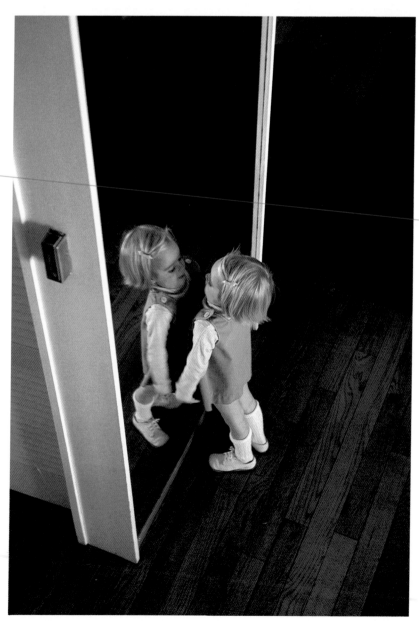

While standing, I could hardly see anything of this baby's face as he lay on the bed. But when I knelt down, I could see his face as well as his body, and the sheet became an important part of the picture.

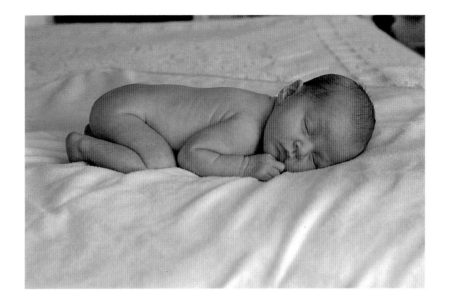

This is another example of a low angle, accompanied by unusual framing: Ira is looking through his father's trouser legs. I was working in a small room and had trouble getting a good picture of the child because someone or something always seemed to be in my way. So I decided to include what I could not ignore. This will often produce a much more lively, realistic shot than will always checking to see if the background or foreground is "clean."

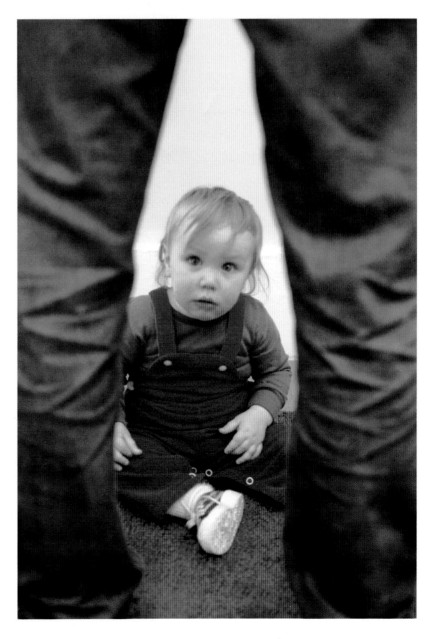

FOREGROUNDS

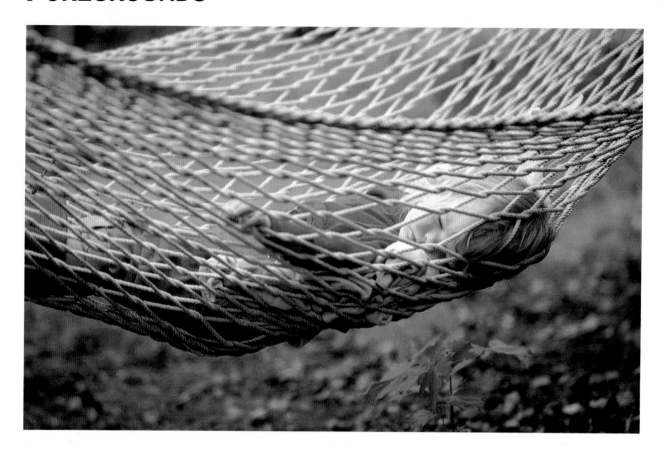

When I saw Maya sleeping in her hammock, I shot several pictures, being careful not to wake her. In the first picture here, I was holding back some branches with my foot in order to get a clear shot of her face. When I let the branches go, I noticed that the greenery added to the feeling of the picture. I kept the foreground blurred, mysterious. "Little blonde Sleeping Beauty in the woods," I thought.

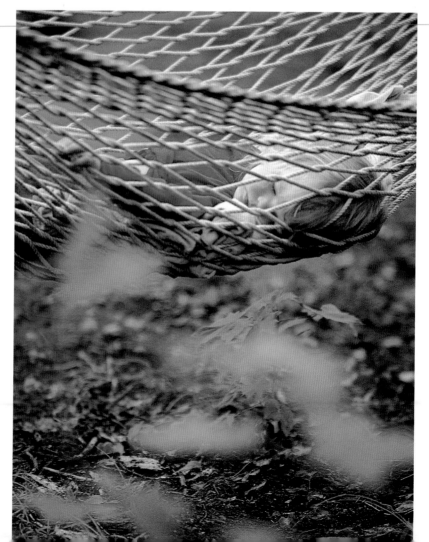

There are two ways to handle the background in your pictures: make it count or play it down by blurring it. In either case, this is an important part of your photograph and can make or break it.

You can control your background by choosing a plain surface to shoot against, one whose color blends into the picture harmoniously. If you cannot find such a background, you can create one by adjusting your lens opening.

You know, of course, that the more you stop down the lens, the greater the depth of field is. Conversely, the more you open the diaphragm, the shallower it becomes. With larger openings, the subject stands out beautifully against a soft, blurry background.

Working with wide openings for out of focus backgrounds, you must remember that exact focusing is vital. Exact focusing means that the most important point in the picture should also be the sharpest; for example, in the case of one child, that point should be the eyes.

The color of any background is also influenced by the amount of light that hits it directly. Unless you aim a light straight at a white wall, it will go gray. Even strong colors can lose their vibrancy if they are not lit adequately.

The focal length of the lens also influences the background in photographs. Long lenses are ideal for blurring the background; wide-angle lenses, for making it sharp and crisp.

The picture in the garden was shot with a 50mm lens, from a distance of three feet, 1/125 sec. at f/2.8.

For the photo of the boy and his dog, I used a 100mm lens, from a distance of six feet, 1/250 sec. at f/2.

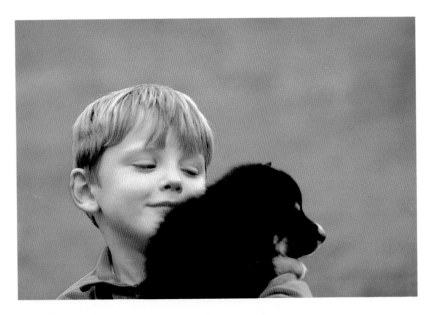

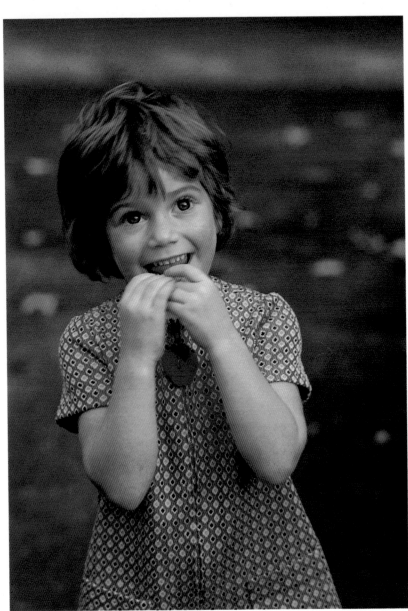

BACKGROUNDS: EMPHASIZED

In these four pictures, I wanted to show the background as clearly as possible. It is the background that sets the stage for the children, giving information about where they are. Obviously, I shot the first two pictures in a big city; the other two, in the country. The city pictures were taken with a 50mm lens, the country photographs with a 35mm lens. In all four photos, I closed the lens down to f/8 and focused on the children.

In the case of travel pictures, you will want to make sure you choose the exposure that will show both the background and foreground clearly.

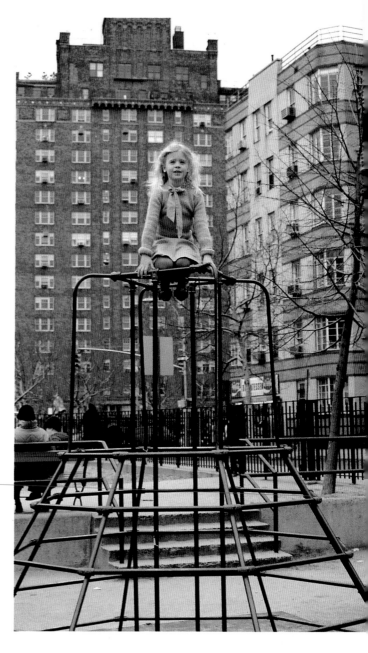

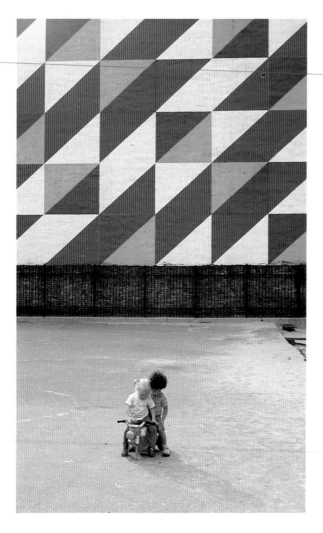

In the photograph of a mother and daughter at the piano, you get a feeling for the atmosphere of their home. Had I been assigned to show the charming antique furniture in detail, I would have had to use additional lighting.

Whenever I evaluate my students in a seminar, I usually end up talking mostly about the way they handle the background in their photographs. I find that they often ignore how it affects their subjects, not only by letting a telegraph pole "grow" out of a

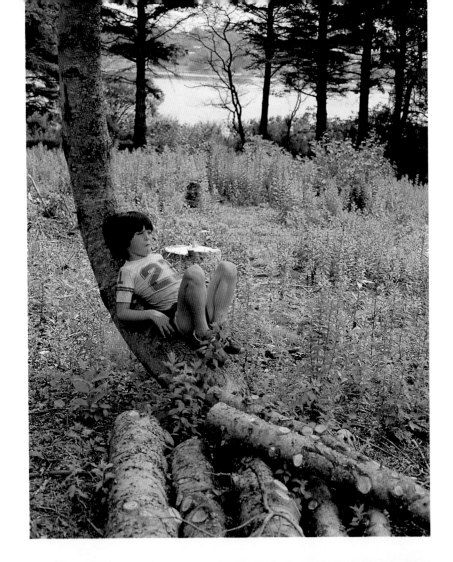

person's head, but also by letting their automatic cameras overemphasize a light background.

My students often fail to use some beautiful element of a landscape to give added meaning to a picture and disregard how the color of the background will affect the foreground.

This is why it is so important to pay careful attention to these points and to be aware of the *f*-stop you are shooting at. Your photographs can improve dramatically if you do.

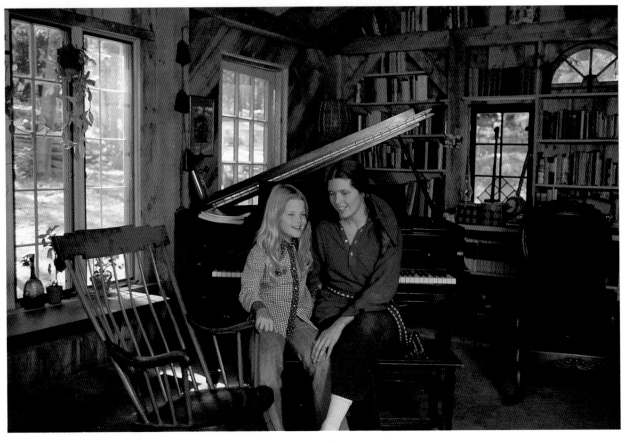

PUTTING
THE BASICS
INTO PRACTICE

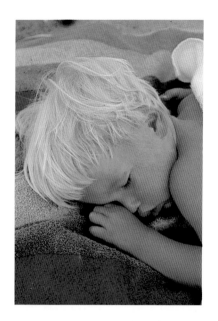

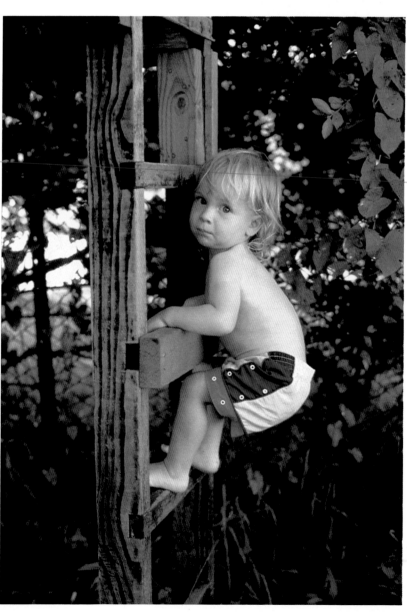

It sounds simplistic but it's true: when you spend time with children, they provide you with one interesting photo challenge after another.

Children are interesting whatever they do; even when eating and drinking (with enthusiasm or reluctance), they look charming. But that is not all. I believe that photographers document all aspects of people's lives, particularly their habits and feelings. For this reason, the simplest everyday photograph may be and often is wanted to illustrate, for example, societal changes, dress habits, or important psychological traits. The photographs in this section show that there are female doctors, that boys wear their hair long in the '80s, and that children can help with lawn work and with preparing muffins.

Small points, to be sure; but from many small points the larger picture emerges: the picture of life around you, which you reinforce with your photography.

(I would like to reiterate my feelings about noting the camera setting and lighting of most of my photographs. About 90 percent of my pictures are taken in very simple ways, and I would be guessing if I tried to give you the exact camera setting in every case. This would also be boring because I took so many of the photographs at 1/100 sec. or 1/60 sec. at $f/4$, $f/5.6$, or $f/8$. This is not one of my quirks; it is sort of an ideal compromise between enough depth of field and fast enough speed that allows me to produce the sharpest picture possible in different situations. It is true, though, that the situations are not *that* diverse. I rarely talk about photographing athletic feats that need very short exposures or large groups that need lots of depth of field—such as $f/8$ to $f/16$. (As I said before, if I used unusual or peculiar exposures, I will mention them.)

I strongly recommend that you get used to photographing in shade. The exposure is closer to that of shooting against the sun than you may think, and the colors glow in a special way. You won't get faces with one side appearing pink and the other brown, depending on where the sun hits, or "average" exposures with automatic cameras unable to bridge the gap.

The photo of the little girl drinking orange juice is a good example of using sunlight properly. By walking around Jane until I found an angle at which the background stayed in the shade and making sure that my exposure was taken from her face, I was able to highlight the juice. After all, I *was* photographing a child drinking her juice.

The picture of Christopher raking the lawn is a semi-silhouette. His body stands out against the background, showing action and enthusiasm. In order to maintain some accurate color in his face and body, I had to over-expose the lawn; shooting from the opposite side would have resulted in better greens, but a less expressive action photo.

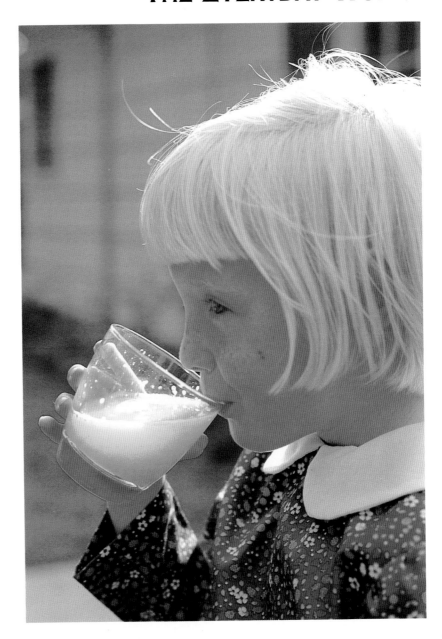

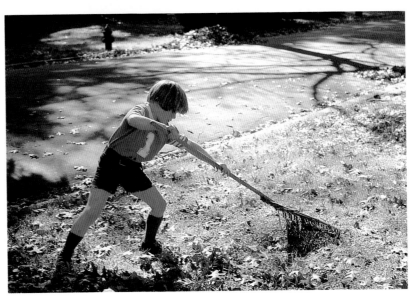

The Everyday World

The three photographs on this page were all shot indoors, with available light, on Ektachrome ISO 200. I believe the exposure was 1/30 sec. at f/4. I am often tempted to use ISO 400 or even faster film, which would let me shoot at 1/60 sec. or even 1/100 sec. (at the same f-stops I usually use). But I have found a difference when it comes to enlarging, projecting, or reproducing these transparencies: more grain, less sharpness.

I followed Peter's mother as she went to wake him up and I saw him, framed by the crib's bars, looking hopeful and adorable. I found Emilia getting dressed by herself. Not many photographers would start their day looking for such everyday occurrences. Still, with very little or no additional light, it is possible to catch these typical scenes of family life.

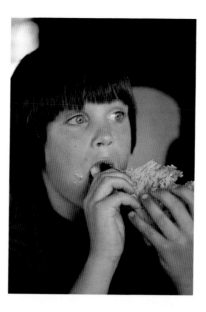

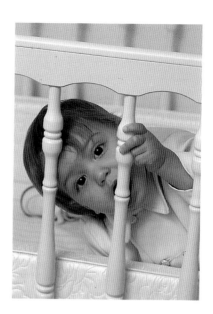

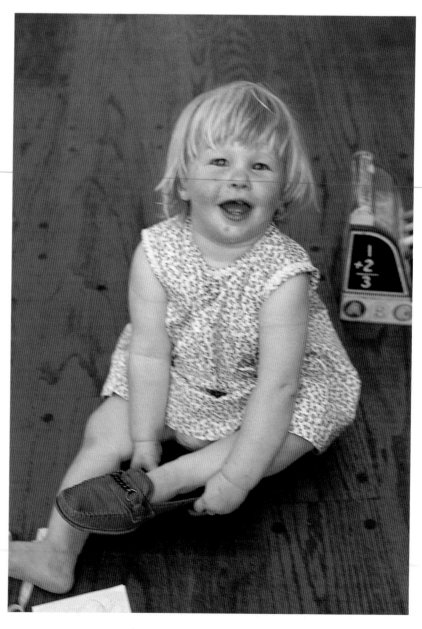

The simple solution to this problem is to add some portable light; in the case of these two photographs, I used a small automatic electronic flash, bounced from the ceiling. Bathrooms are especially suitable for this method; they are usually small and white and add two *f*-stops to the exposure. But beware! Only a few cameras will synchronize at faster than 1/60 sec. We are now back at my favorite exposure of 1/60 sec. at *f*/5.6. (See more on fill-in flash on page 22.)

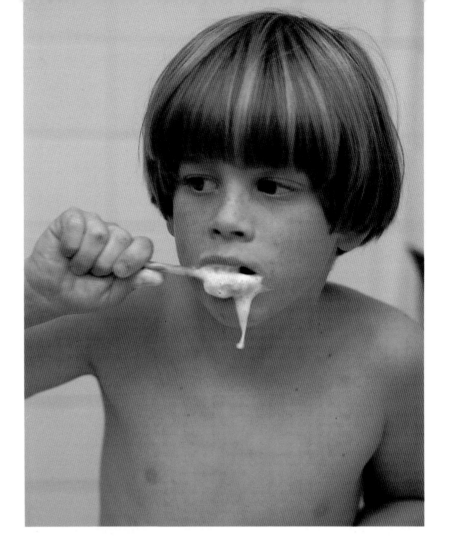

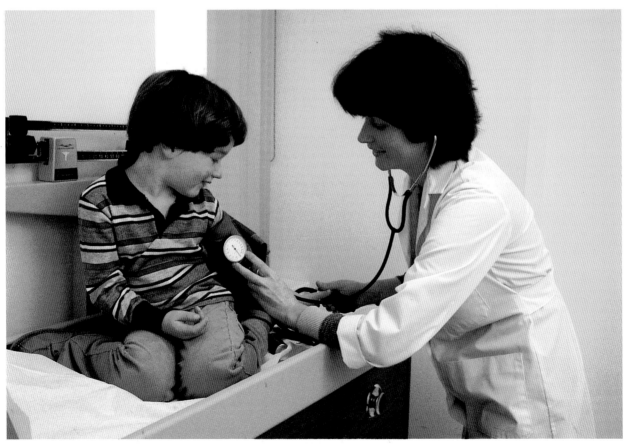

The Everyday World

Of all my photographs, I like those best that have a certain quality of happy accident and intimacy. The longer I plan what I want, the more I lose these qualities. Instead, I like to take advantage of even the smallest incident. In the two photographs on this page, both mothers greeted me with apologies that they weren't ready yet; one child insisted on taking a bath, and the other was still in bed with a cold. The mothers were surprised that I welcomed these situations and felt that they would produce interesting pictures.

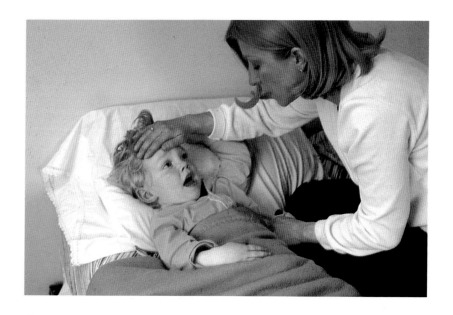

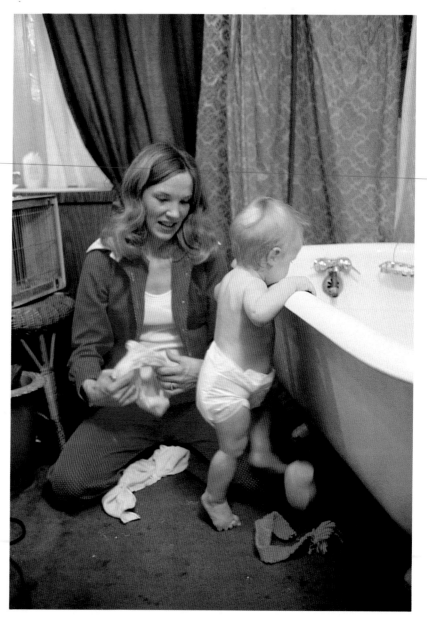

Here are two photographs that show how I use photofloods. I love floods because I can shoot without the interruption of flashing lights and can see what I will get. In the first picture, I used one photoflood on a stand near me, bounced from the ceiling and Ektachrome ISO 160 tungsten-balanced film. The second picture was a bit more tricky. I used daylight film but emphasized the background by clamping a flood on a convenient shelf.

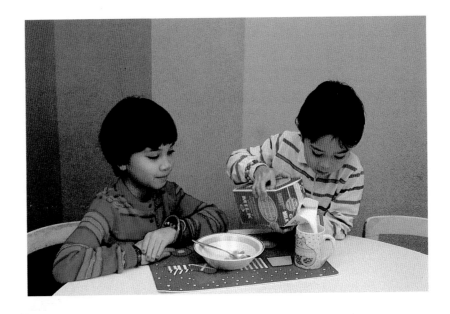

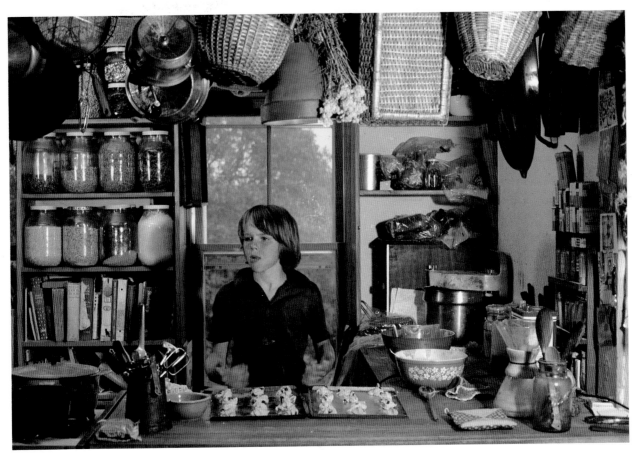

COLOR AND CONTENT

Obviously, a fine color photograph will owe its excellence to both its content and the beauty of its colors. But you rarely encounter the best of both worlds, and generally either content or artistic color will predominate.

Sometimes color can spoil an otherwise excellent picture. Some subjects cry out for somber colors and subdued light. Imagine a scene of a very poor, forlorn child wearing a torn, bright orange dress, shot against a clear blue sky. Between the gaiety of the colors and the sadness of the child, you get conflicting messages.

You could blame the photographer's taste: the colors seem to trivialize the content. But what can the photographer do other than not take the picture? He or she cannot control the color of the subject's dress nor make the sky turn gray by wishing it. If the photographer is able to change position, the sky could be eliminated and the pavement could become the background.

Sometimes luck is with me. The little girl in this picture used paint exactly the same color as her dress. Her evident dedication to her task contributes to the satisfying feeling the photograph evokes.

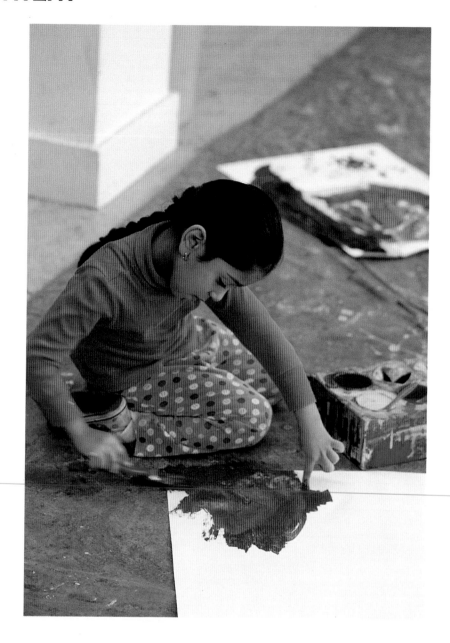

This picture of a little boy sucking his thumb was taken at a beach. The late afternoon sun produced the lovely, warm skin tones; here, the colors enhance the value.

Sometimes you have so little time to take a picture that you almost have to shoot without a thought to improving it. This quarrel erupted so quickly and the teachers were so close, ready to intervene, that I barely got this one shot. The overflowing emotion of the two children gives this picture its value.

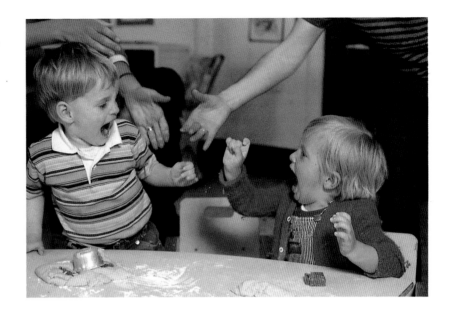

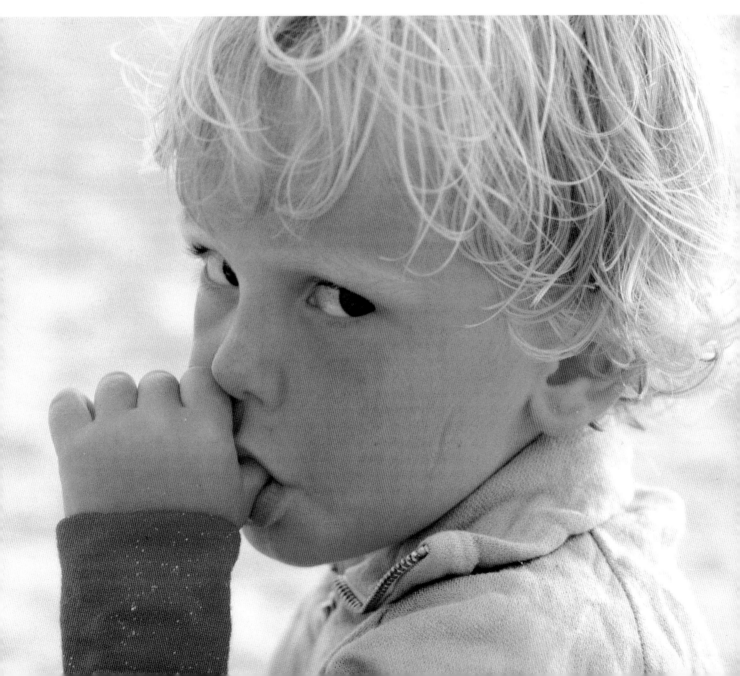

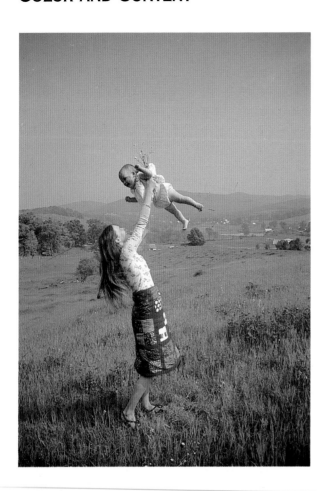

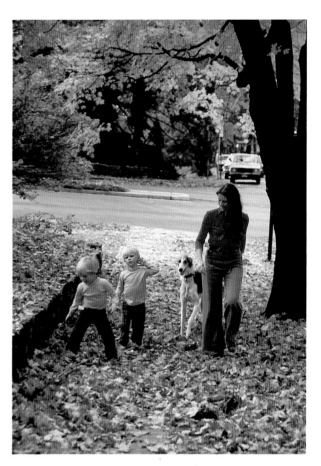

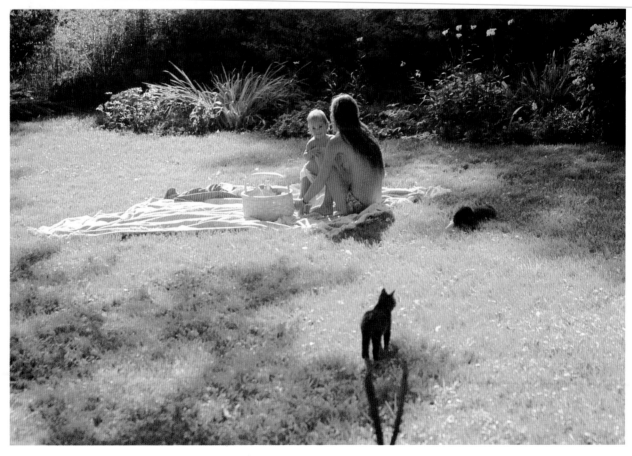

Here are three photographs of mothers and children enjoying the outdoors. What would nature be without green meadows, golden leaves, and blue skies? No black-and-white film could match color here. The colors seem to echo the subjects' enjoyment of breathing fresh air while playing, of having fun with a pet, and of this beauty.

A brief note about gilding the lily: when I started to photograph my friend playing with her baby in the Vermont hills, she was wearing a blue denim skirt. After a while, I asked her to tie the baby's quilted red blanket around her waist—a definite improvement.

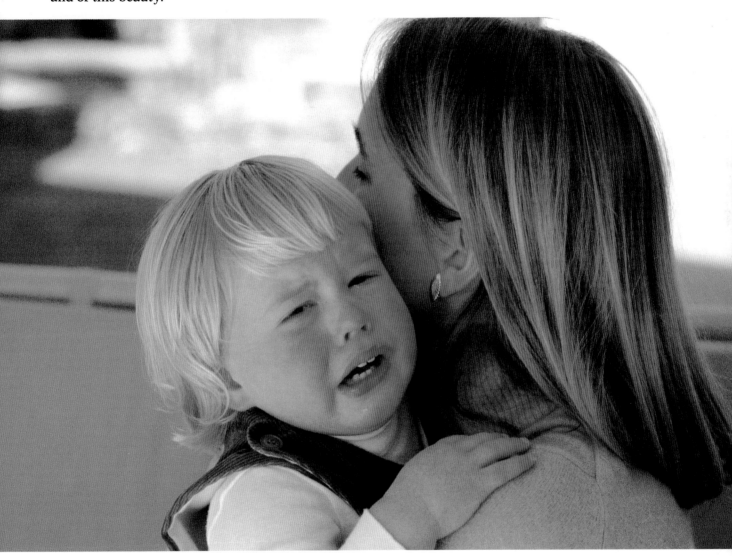

This photograph would be just as good in black and white. I wanted to catch the child's distress. If anything, without the nice colors, the content would become more striking.

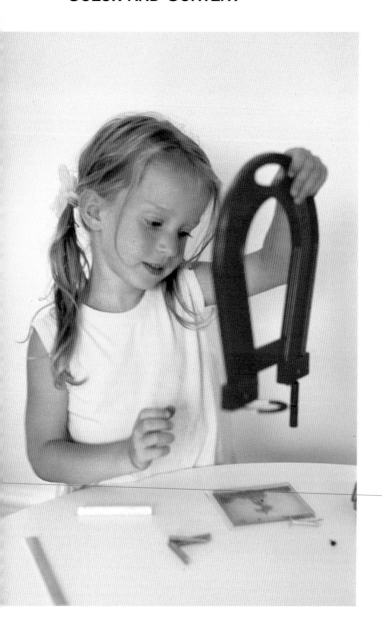

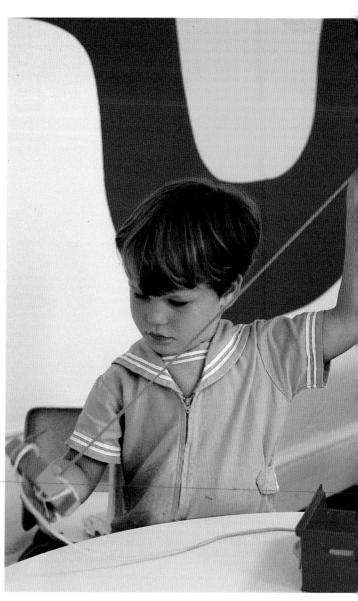

I am tempted to put together the two photographs in which the curve of the big red magnet is repeated in the wall decoration of the nursery school. This color-as-design can keep you from looking at other aspects of the picture, such as whether or not the children are really absorbed in their work, for instance. (I used an 85mm lens so they wouldn't be aware of me.)

The color white can look brilliant when lit by enough light, or it can look dark gray, as in the kitchen wall in the background of this photo.

If you have ever observed the color of flowers in a garden at dusk, you will have noticed how colors lose their saturation and become darker and darker.

The picture below is an example of an appropriate background. The sight of falling leaves is melancholy, and these children are not happy.

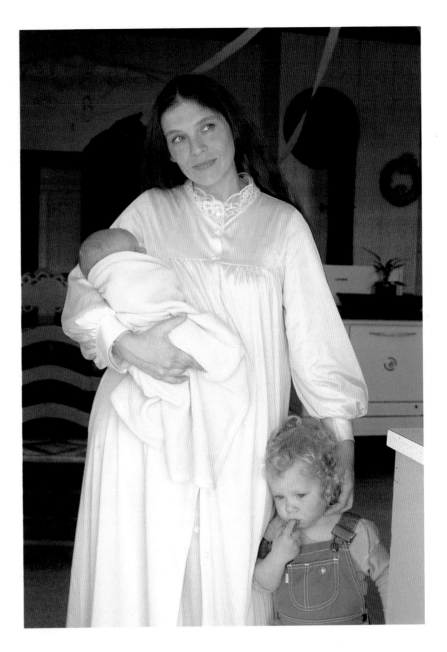

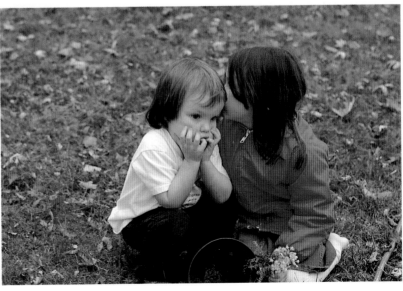

COLOR VERSUS BLACK AND WHITE

What is the difference between black-and-white and color photographs? Do different films have distinct personalities? Are there any rules about when you use one or the other? Hard questions with only tentative answers.

The difference between black-and-white and color photography is that black and white is much less literal than color. Obviously, all photographs are abstractions since, to begin with, they are two-dimensional. And few photographs, except in specialized fields, are the actual size of what is represented. Then, when we translate color into a set of tones ranging from black through gray to white, we have again moved farther away from reality. Thus, through photos we re-experience reality, minus three of its basic characteristics.

As for film itself, it is not so much that each has its own personality, but that photographers choose, for conscious or unconscious reasons, the film that fits their personality.

I rarely feel like taking the very same picture in black and white and color, but with this photo I did. My black-and-white picture of the mother and her two children is the better one, I think. Why did it turn out this way?

In the first few minutes of shooting in black and white, all I concentrated on was the mother-son-baby trio, and I captured something of its psychological possibilities: the older child's tension as he waits to be given his breakfast.

In general, color film makes both the photographer and the viewer concentrate on the outward attributes of a scene. We look at the shiny copper bowl and notice the green leaves of the plants. Thus distracted, the photographer may miss the right instant to click the shutter and show subjects at their most interesting.

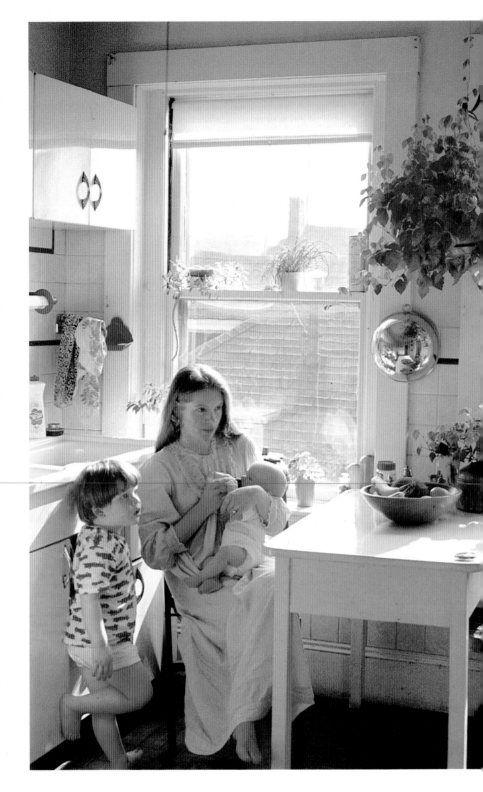

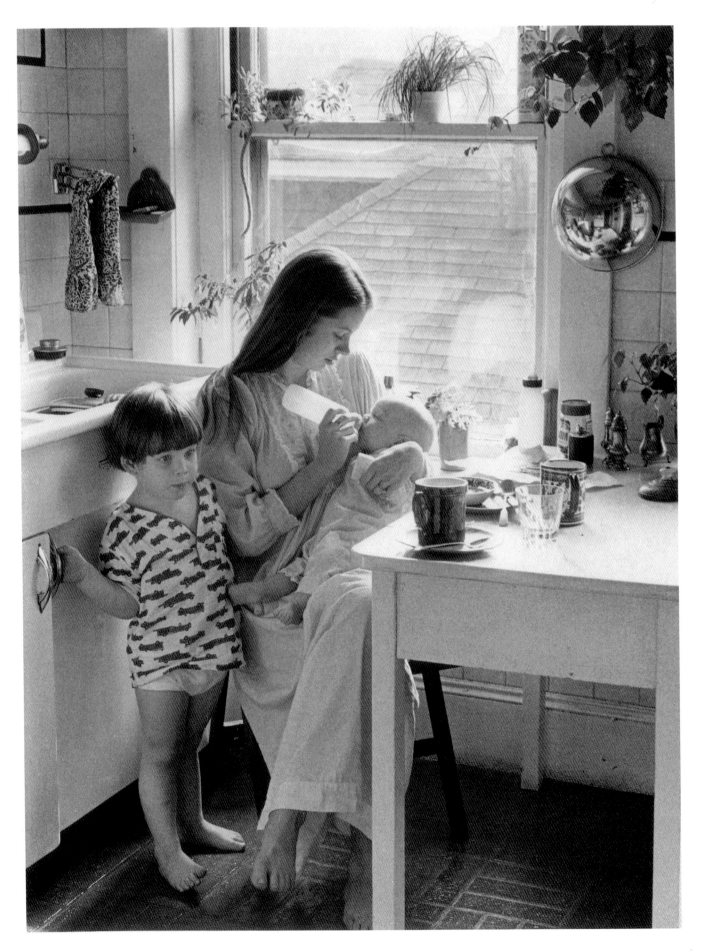

PHOTOGRAPHING IN BLACK AND WHITE

Transforming real life—which has color—into black-and-white photographs—in which shades of gray represent color—is very exciting. With black and white, you are not forced to choose between color or content; your attention—and, as a result, your camera—is focused on your subject. You feel that, by distancing yourself from reality, you have created something new, something magical.

You also learn a lot by handling black and white. Developing; making contact prints; and learning to wash, dry, number, enlarge, crop, and mount: all this is eliminated when you entrust most of this work to a lab, as is done with color transparencies. As a result, I somehow feel that I know my black-and-white photographs much better than I do my little color transparencies.

I have also found that parents really appreciate a good black-and-white portrait or action shot of their children; they rarely can produce one themselves.

A final point: museums still show mostly black-and-white prints. It is much more rare to find color photography—now the accepted medium for magazines, television, and advertising—accepted as art.

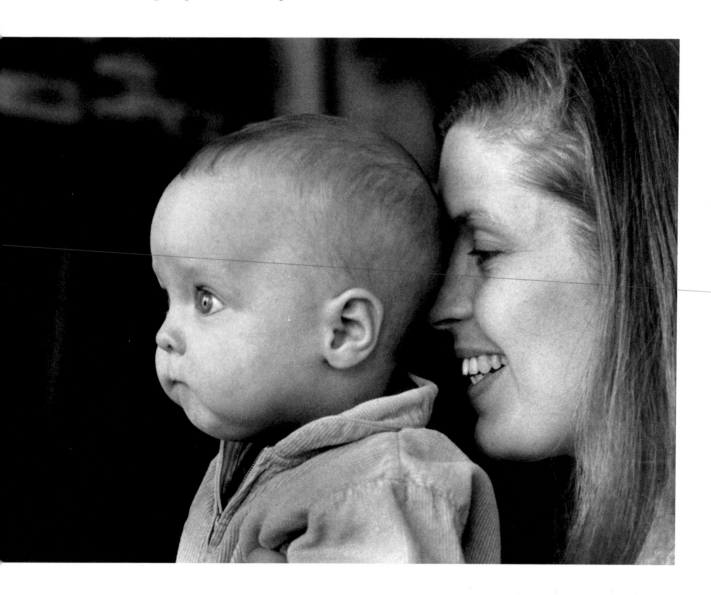

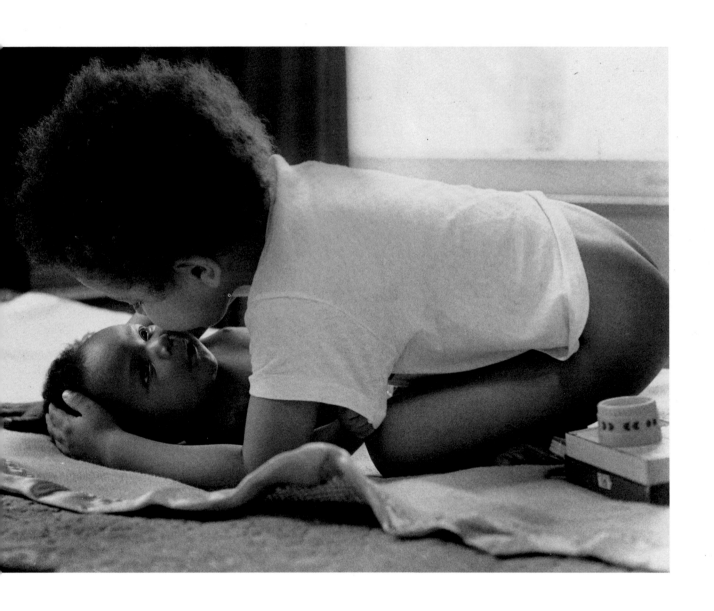

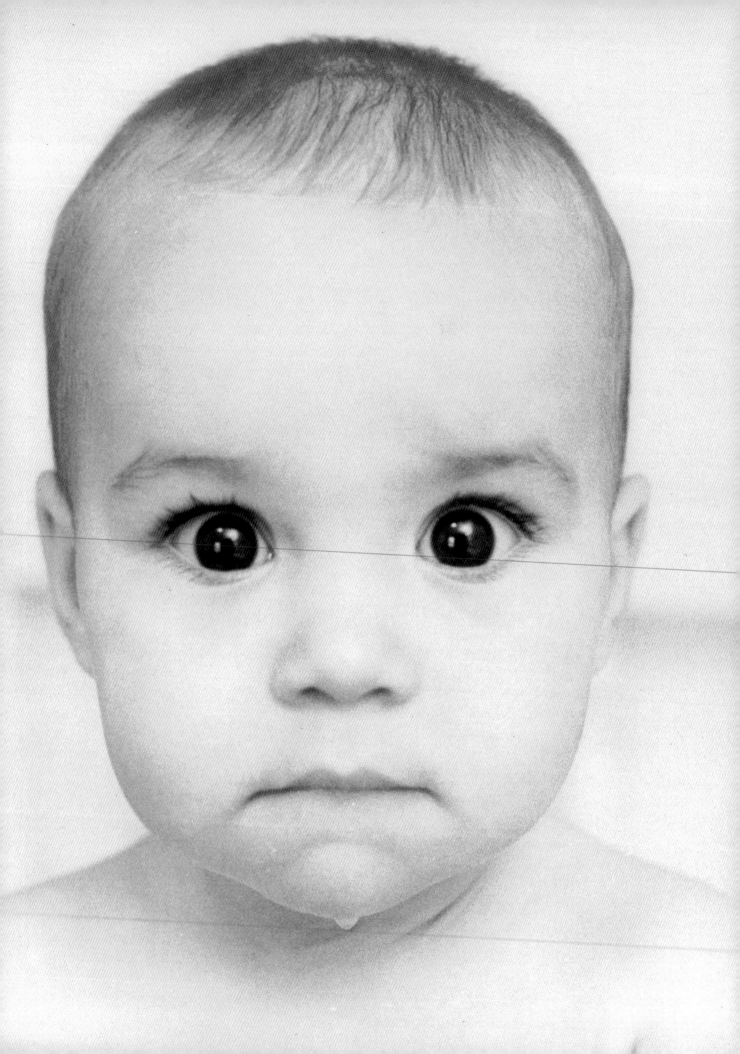

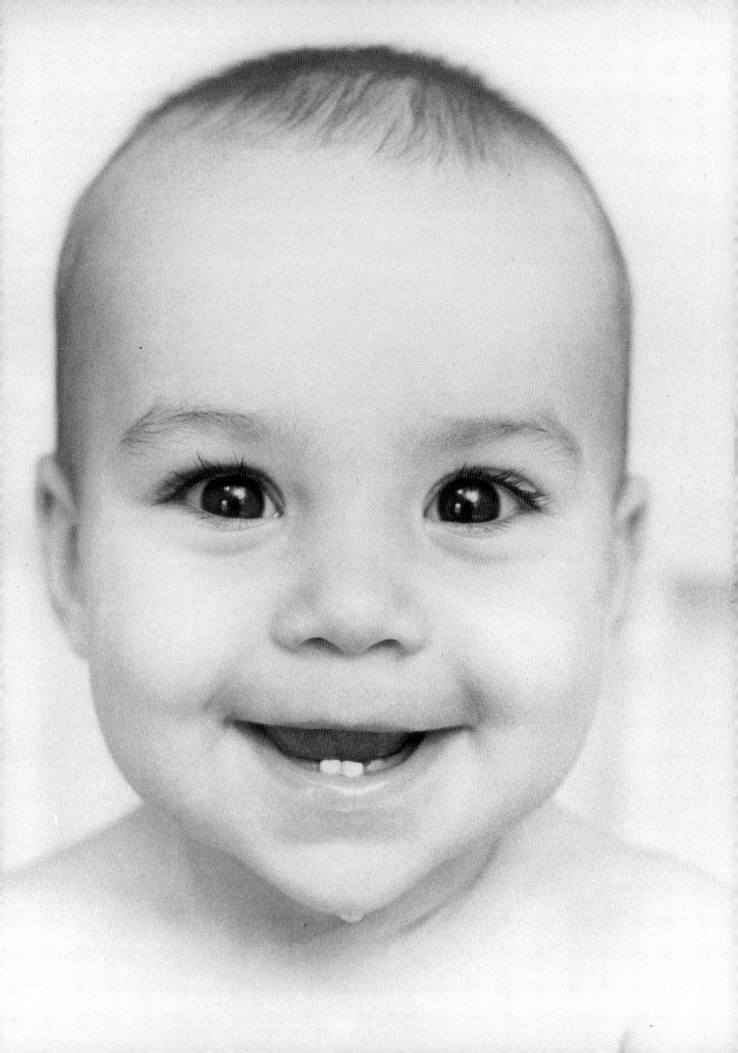

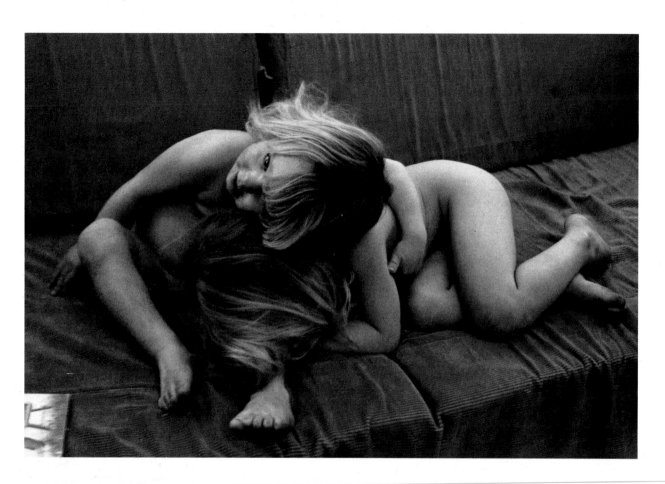

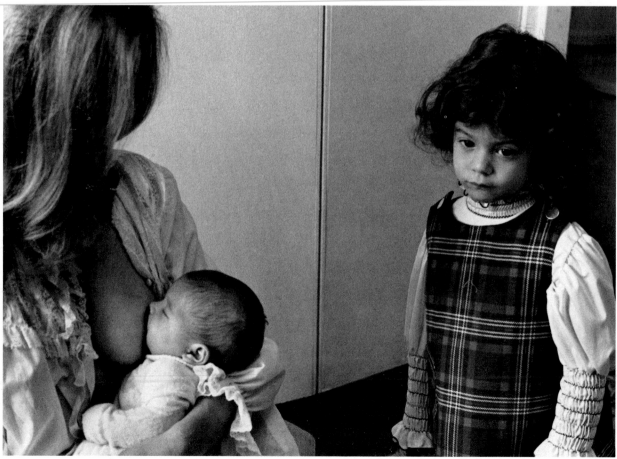

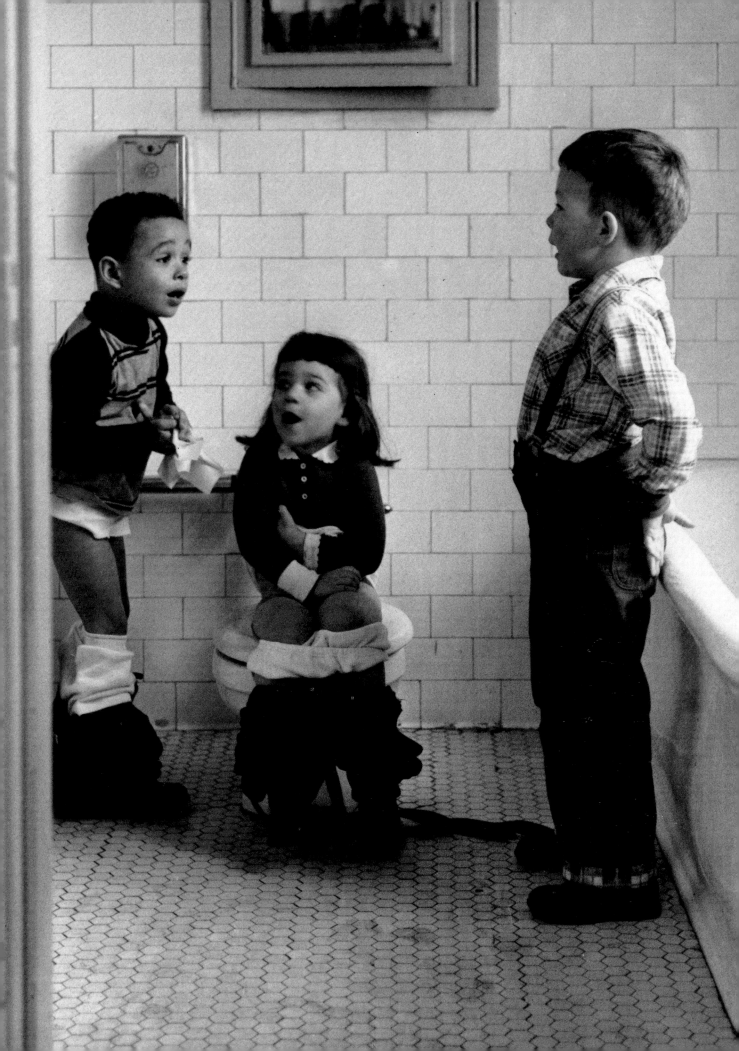

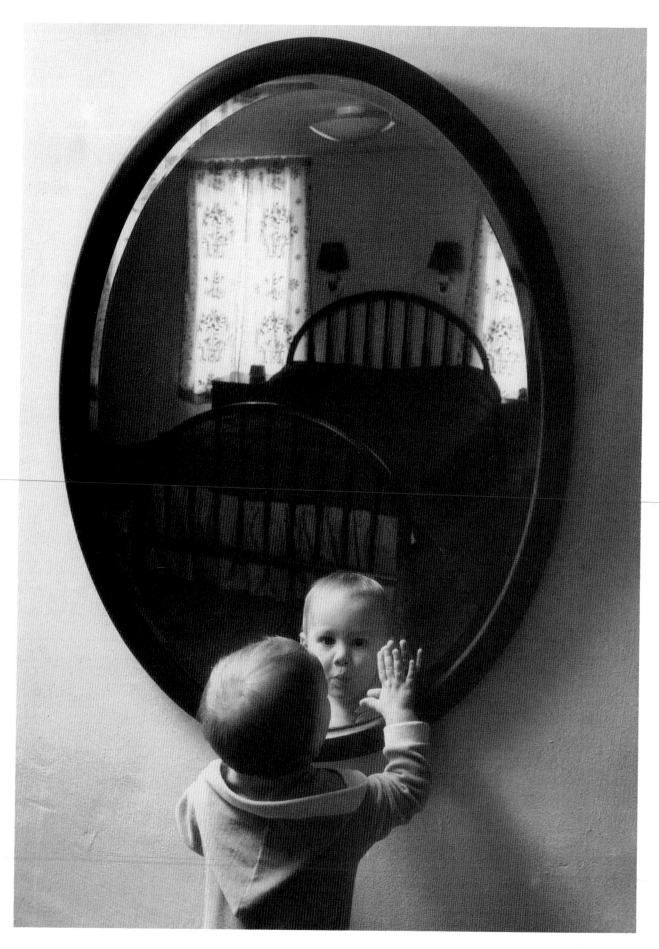

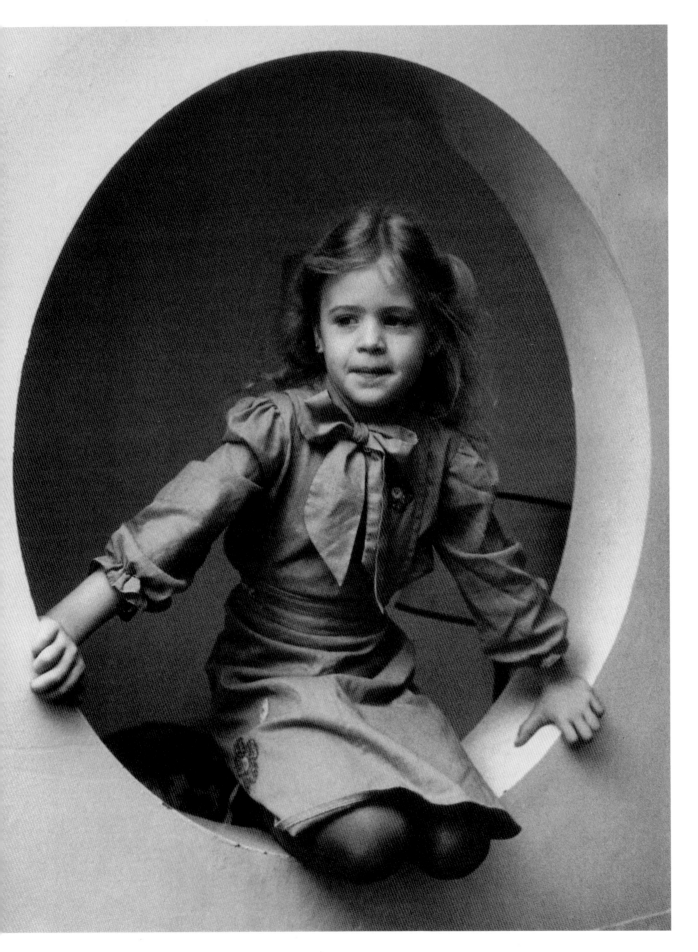

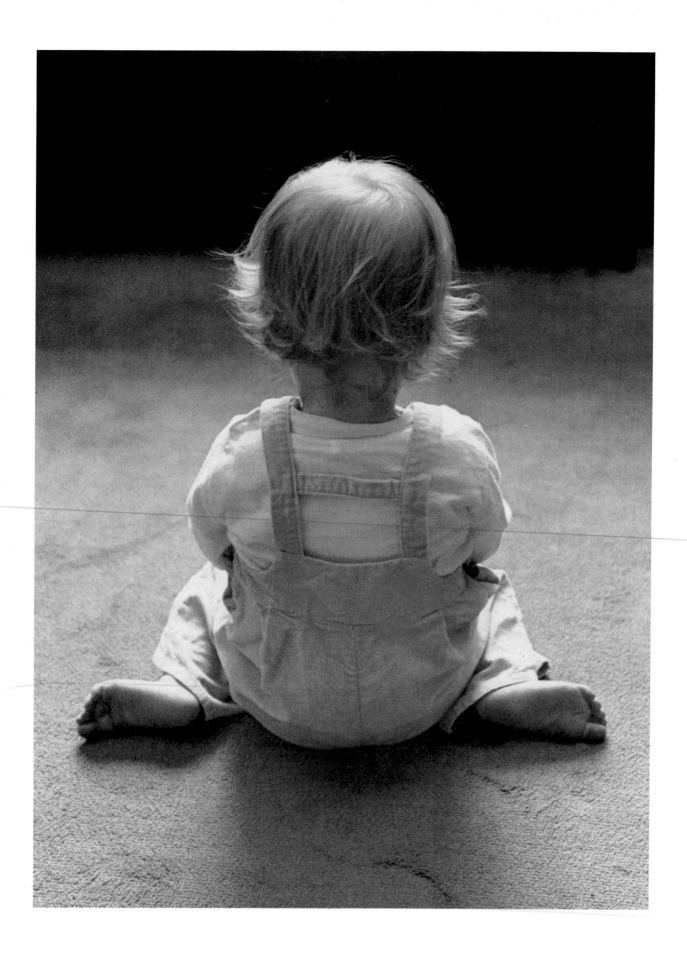

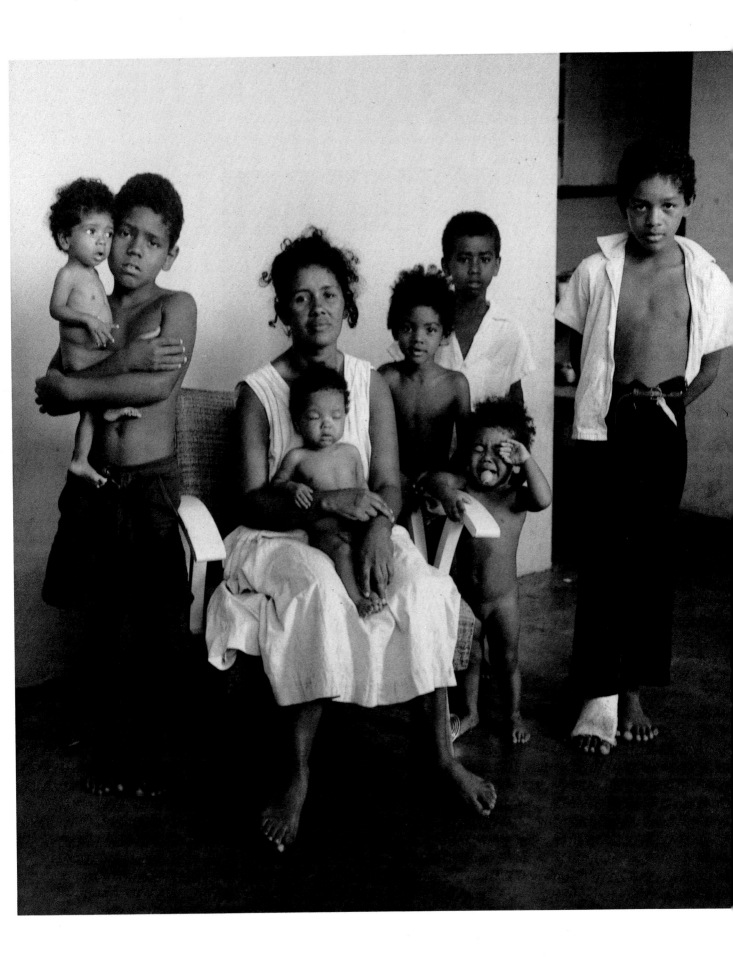

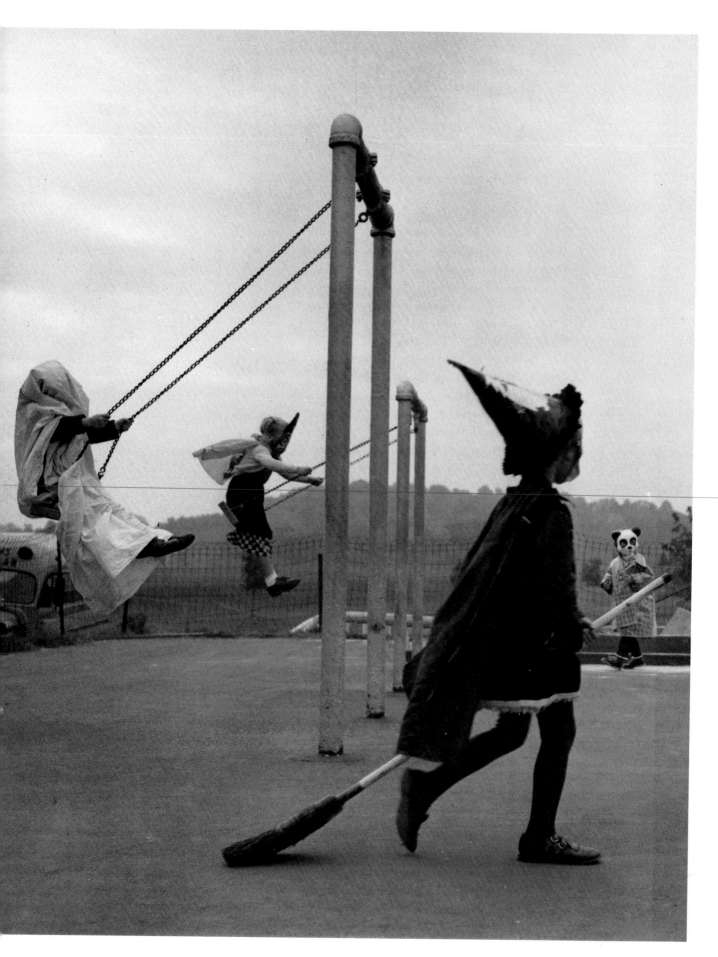

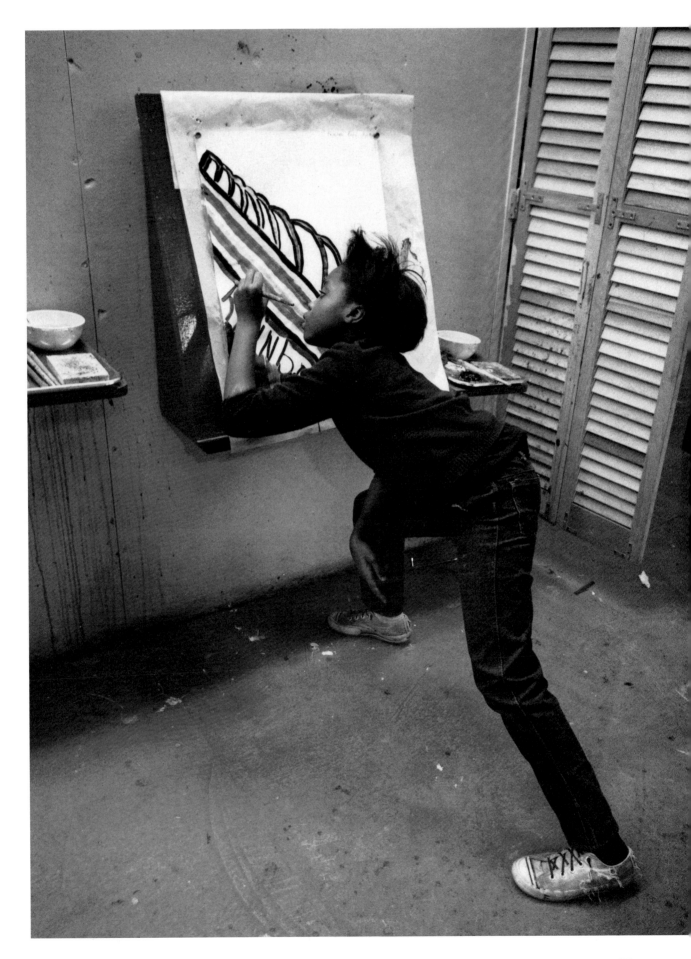

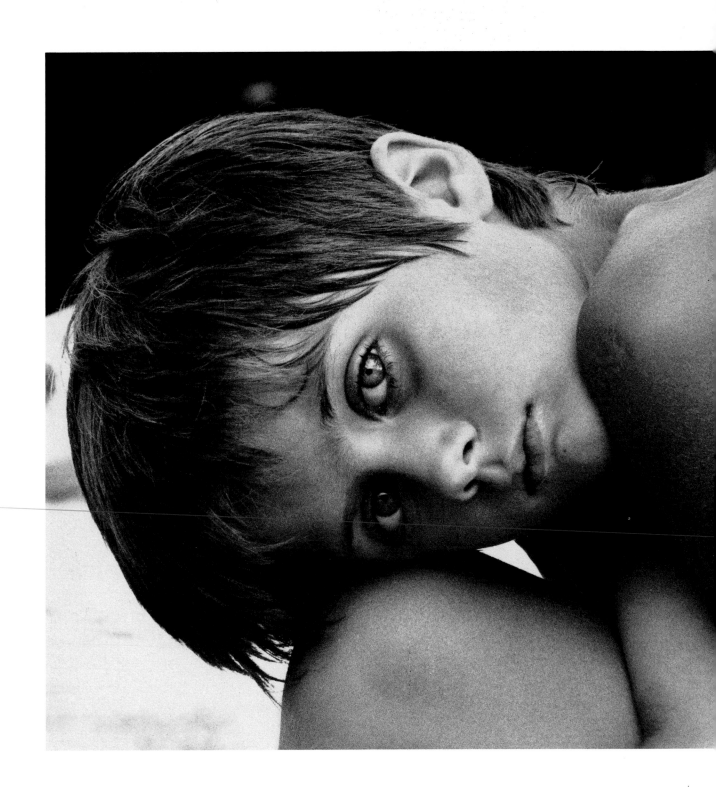

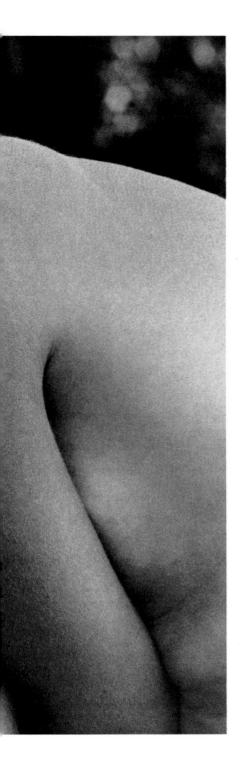

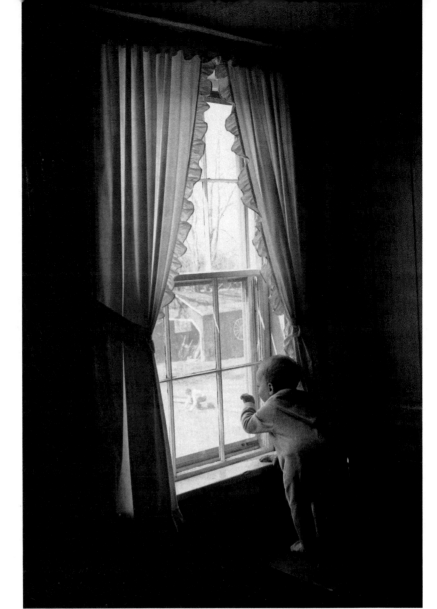

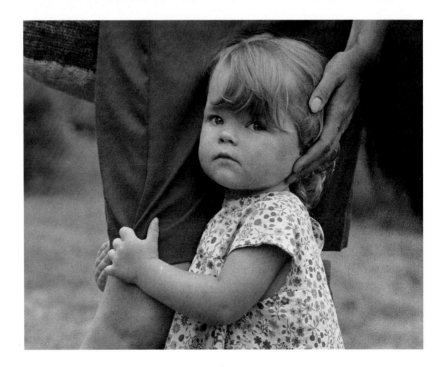

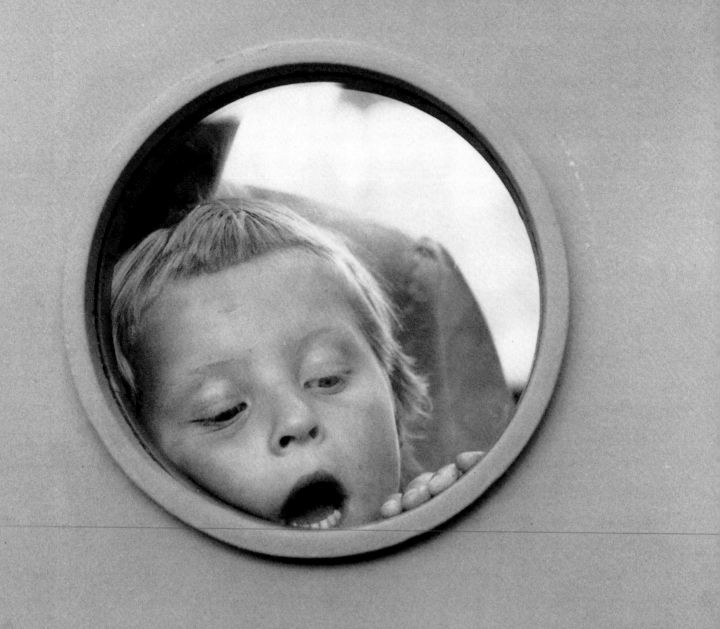

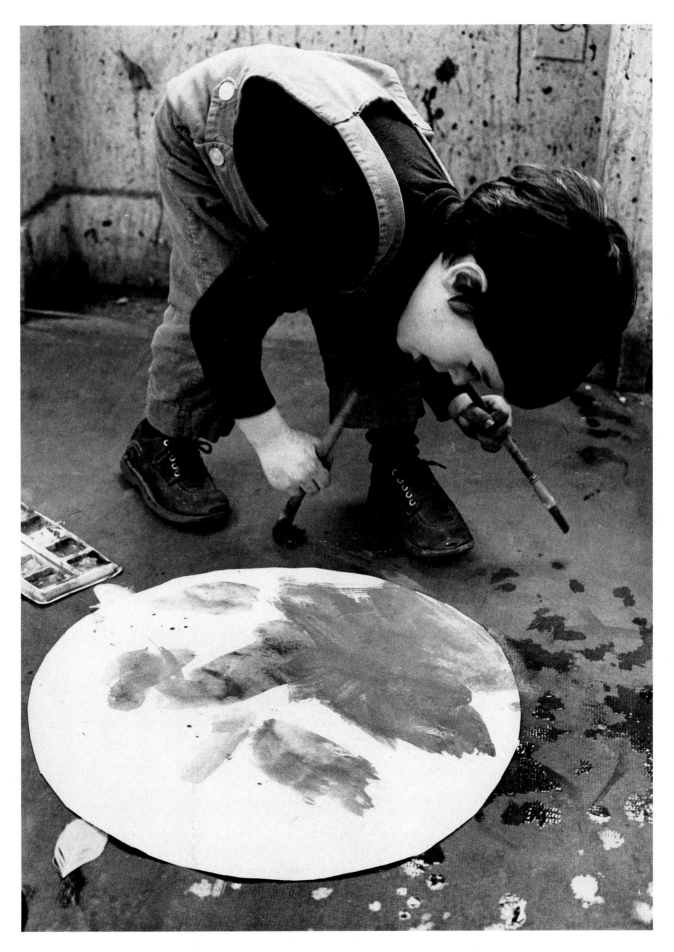

PORTRAITS

I have read many different definitions of what a portrait is. Some think it is an image of a face; for others, the classical painted portrait comes to mind: people on their best behavior posed in their best clothes. Still others believe that the background should be included in the picture. But is an unposed head shot a portrait?

I would answer "yes"—especially when it comes to children—about any photograph showing the subject as he or she really is. Head shots, posed or unposed; head and shoulders, in a bubble bath, eyes looking at the camera or looking away; and even eyes cast down. The children's expressions range from serious to sad to funny. They can be comfortable or shy before the camera; they can hide or show off. Their hair can be carefully combed or blowing in the breeze. The children can be bundled up for a cold day of skating or dressed up for the school play. They can do just about anything as long as it is what the children really are or do at this time in their lives.

Children enjoy looking at their photographs even at an early age. A two-year-old will point at himself and say proudly, "Baby!" Later, he goes back to look at the photographs just as he likes to hear the same story over and over again. He feels appreciated and important: the star of the photo album.

This is why it is important for parents to appreciate photographs of their children in all moods, sad and serious as well as cheerful and happy. The pictures give children the kind of acceptance they need. After all, the children, who know that they are not always happy, like to see that their parents accept and value their serious expressions, too.

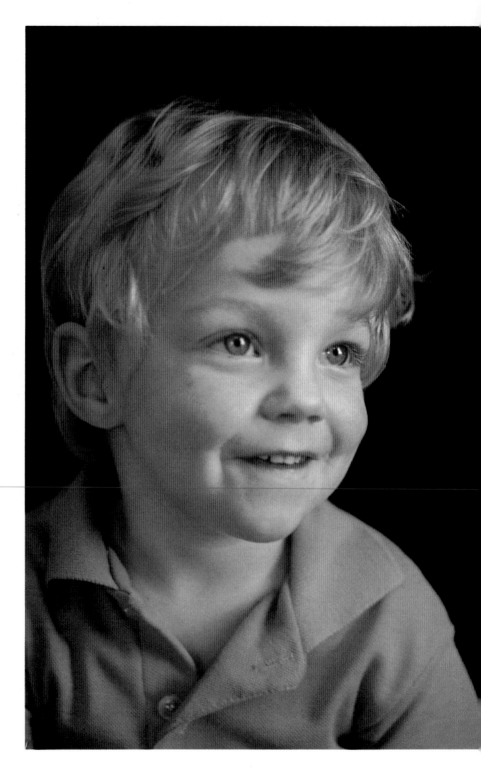

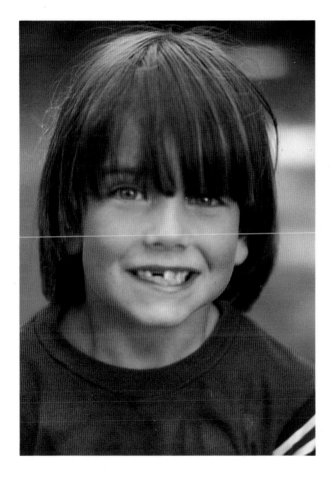
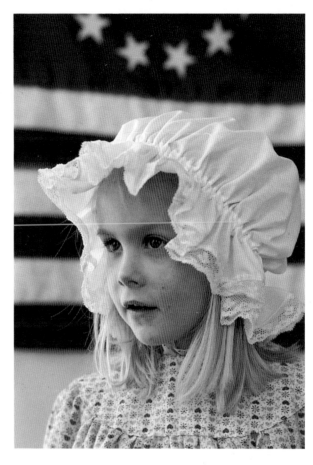
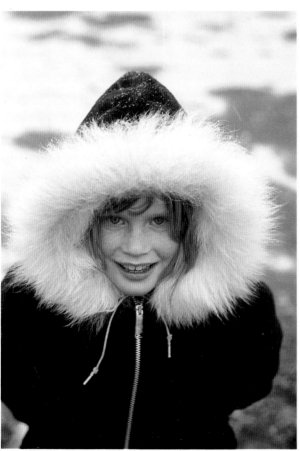
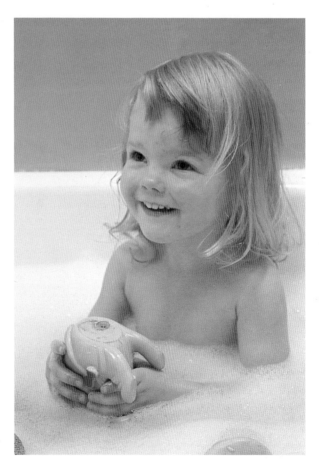

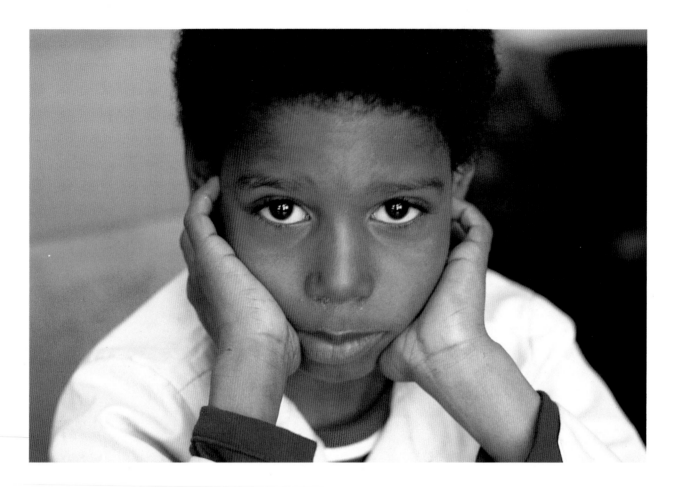

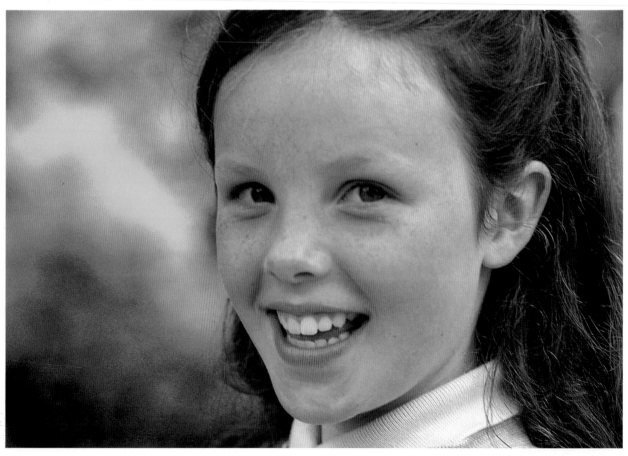

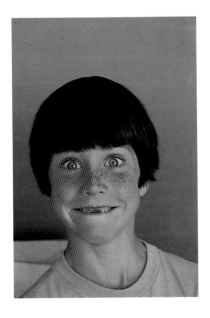

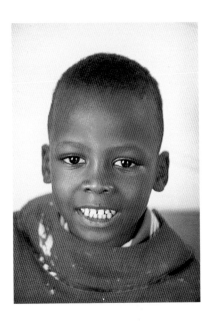

All but two of the portraits in this section were taken with a long lens and are reproduced here full frame.

If you want to fill out the frame by using a normal or a wide-angle lens, you have to get extremely close to your subjects. This not only distorts their features but often makes them very uncomfortable. With my 35mm Minoltas, I use either an 85mm, 100mm, or 135mm lens with little distress and great success.

An added bonus: these lenses are quite easy to focus because their depth of field is shallow. This, in turn, gives you the advantage of blurring the background. Disadvantages? I can think of two. First, the lenses are larger and heavier to carry. Second, you must be sure to focus correctly (always on the eyes, please!) in order to produce a sharp image. There are many fine zoom lenses that will give you the same possibilities.

You may already have noticed that I choose soft, even light whenever I can. I also create it by using bounced lights.

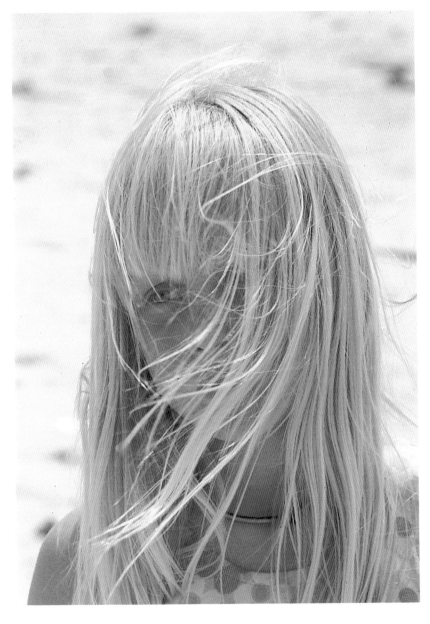

BABIES, BABIES, BABIES

You need not be a child psychologist to photograph children, but it helps to know a bit about their development. Once I started to read books on the subject, I was so fascinated I couldn't stop. I learned about the phases children go through, such as the fear of strangers that affects most of them around their eighth month. It helps to know this when you are going to photograph a child that age. You will be aware that you should not suddenly approach or touch a baby, however lovingly. You should also avoid remaining alone with the baby; its sense of security depends on its mother.

I like to have the parents around anyway. I find that the children then continue to be themselves—and to act as if I were not there at all. They respond to the people they are used to and are less interested in me and my camera. I won't deny that I have met mothers and fathers who continually admonish their child not to suck his or her thumb or squirm or wrinkle new clothes because "we want nice pictures of you." In such cases, it is better to go to a playground where the child can relax.

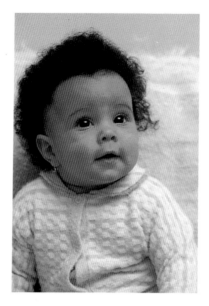

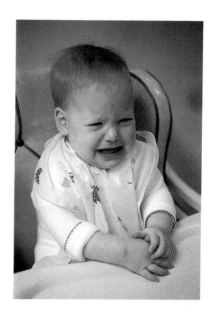

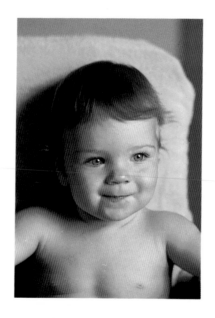

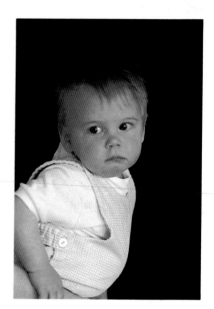

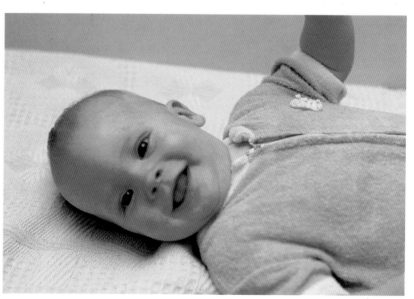

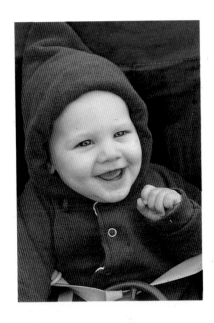
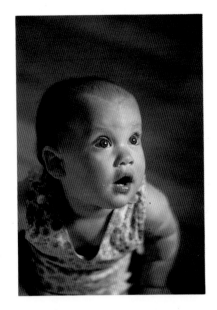
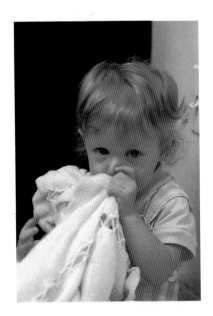
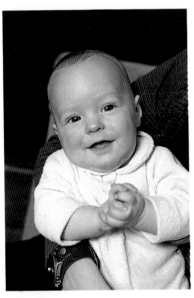
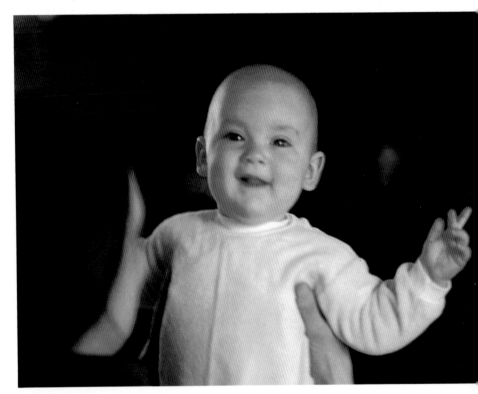
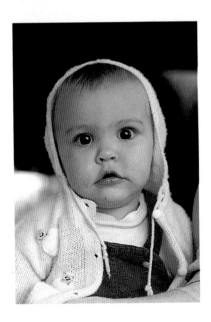
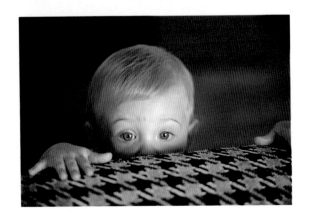

CHILDREN AT DIFFERENT AGES

There is a good reason why children about 18 months old or so are called the "Terrible Twos." You never know what will cause a temper tantrum! But you *can* turn the tables on these little firecrackers: ask them to do the opposite of what you want. I may say, "Could you show me those kicks you just did, but much faster?" Or, "I would like to take a sad picture of you. Don't smile!"

These tricks usually work, but in general, the best strategy is just to ignore the children for a few minutes and let them do what they really want to do.

Children about the age of four are fascinated by the camera and the way it works. Do not allow them to take a peek in the viewfinder; they won't want to give you back your equipment and may even hurt it.

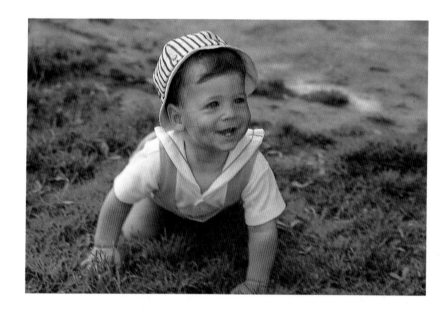

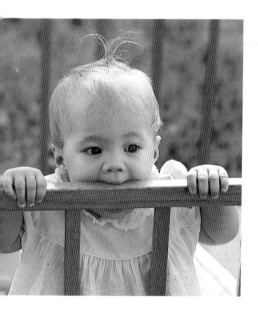

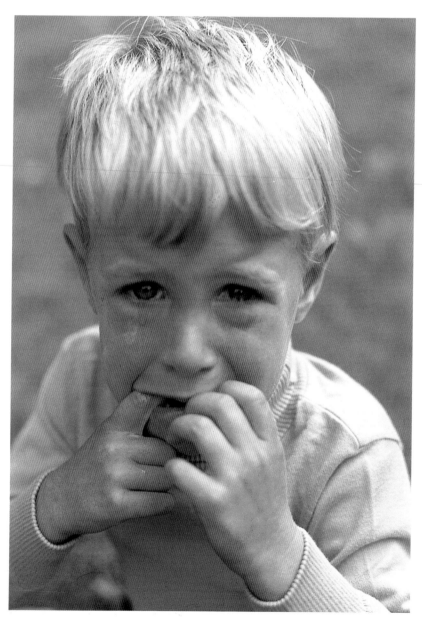

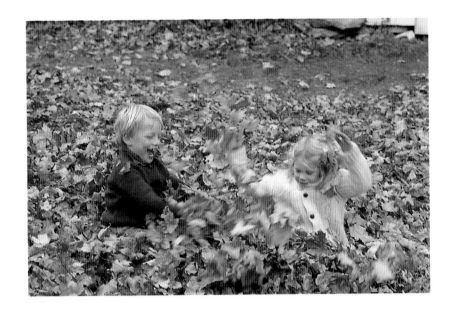

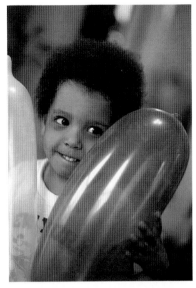

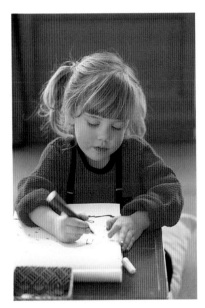

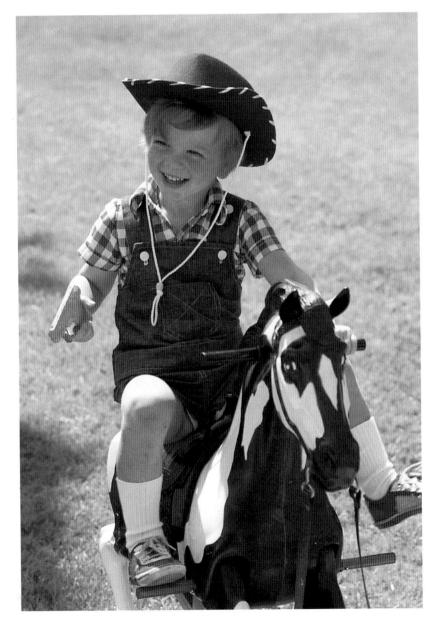

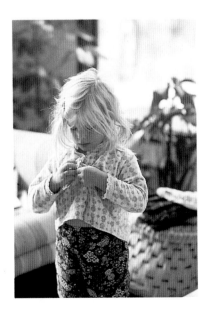

CHILDREN AT DIFFERENT AGES

I seem to have few problems photographing children because anything they do interests me and seems to be good photographic material. I also think that children have a special beauty—including the few little monsters among them.

I cannot think of anything sadder than a child who has so little self-confidence that he or she is truly reluctant to be photographed. This lack of confidence is particularly prevalent at the start of puberty. These children worry greatly about their looks. Sometimes only one method works: shoot them in groups (of the same sex, of course!) or at least with their best friends.

Teenagers may not have outgrown this phase. Instead of acting naturally, they pose, imitate their teen idols, and can make your work difficult at times.

THE DIFFERENT STAGES OF CHILD DEVELOPMENT

Age	Activity	How It Affects Photographer
First weeks	Smiles when stimulated	Have parents close to infant
1 to 2 mos.	Grasps hand or toy	Show how infant discovers the world
5 to 7 mos.	Crawls	Learn to move fast
5 to 9 mos.	Sits up	Take advantage of easy portrait shots
About 8 mos.	May be scared of strangers	Let parent handle baby, and don't move or touch baby suddenly
9 to 12 mos.	Stands up	Baby needs support (child stays in one place for a while)
10 to 18 mos.	Learns to walk. Learns to feed and dress itself	Try to catch the early days, when the child holds on to thin air (later it walks back and forth between its parents)
18 mos.	Starts the "Terrible Twos" period	Persuade parents that pictures of this phase will retain their interest when one more smile will be forgotten
1 yr.	Learns more this year than in any other year of its life	Show all this learning, with all its frustrations and triumphs
2 yrs.	Learns to cope with a sibling	Take dramatic pictures of jealousy
3 to 4 yrs.	Goes off to nursery school	Follow child if you can get permission from the school
6 to 12 yrs.	Enters the least chronicled years	Keep on shooting
12 yrs.	Enters preadolescence	Shoot in a group if child resists because of lack of confidence
15 yrs.	Enters adolescence	Discover and document this fascinating, contradictory period
At any time	Wants only to be outdoors, preferably on wheels or up a tree	Get comfortable shoes and a long lens

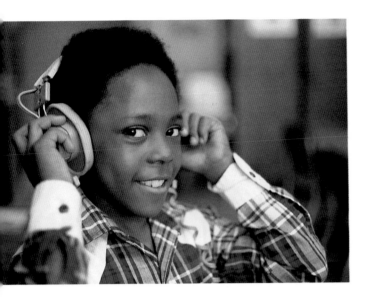

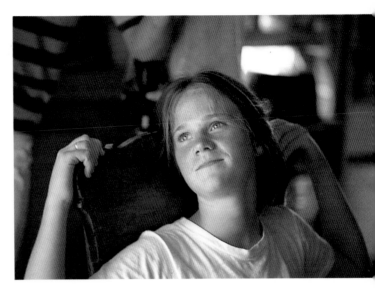

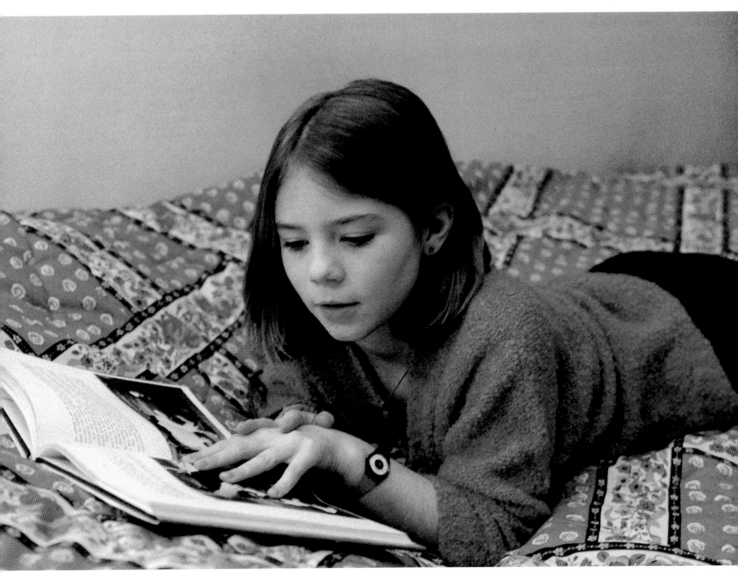

MORE THAN ONE

Taking a picture of two children can be half the trouble of photographing one child. At least this is true for someone like me, who likes it so much more when life simply goes on wherever I work. So, if two children are playing and having fun, I only have to make sure that I don't interrupt them.

There is a way of behaving that ensures this. I walk very slowly and softly and wear rubber-soled shoes. I don't talk unless absolutely necessary. I handle my camera casually, and I don't unpack all my equipment at once, which would draw attention to this fascinating assemblage. I don't seek eye contact with the children. In fact, I sometimes pretend to be photographing something or someone else, thus reassuring my real subjects.

Whenever I show my photographs or teach, the first question that I'm usually asked is: "How do you make friends with the children?" My answer: "I don't." I want them to ignore me and continue what they were doing before. This is why I shun studios, where it is so much harder to recreate what happens naturally in any home: family members eating together, children building with their blocks, babies crying—scores of interesting situations. All you have to do is to keep out of the way.

When two or more children are together, you are much less tempted to "make friends." And if you don't try to direct your subjects, you will have more time to develop the kind of sensitivity that can anticipate a kiss or a blow. You will be able to change your vantage point to gain the best background: to lie practically flat on the floor or to perch on a ledge or a wooden chair. You will also have time to bracket the exposure (automatic camera or

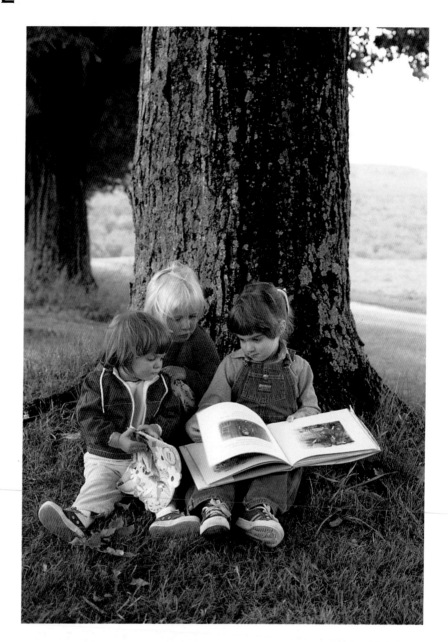

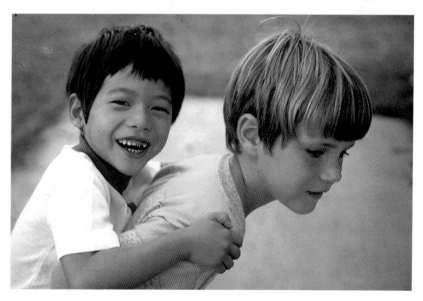

not), to change lenses, and to make notes.

It took me a while to realize that nearly all the "more than one" photographs I had chosen from my files are of siblings. I had been pursuing this subject for a long time, and in 1984 a book of my black-and-white photographs, which I wrote with Elizabeth Taleporos, was published: *Sisters, Brothers, and Others* (New York: W. W. Norton & Company, Inc., 1984). I had accumulated many color shots as well.

There is something special about sisters and brothers. Their deep feelings of love alternate with moments of jealousy and rejection.

There is nothing special about the technical aspects of the photographs in this section. You already know that I avoid the sun most of the time; when I see thick, white clouds, I am off to shoot in color.

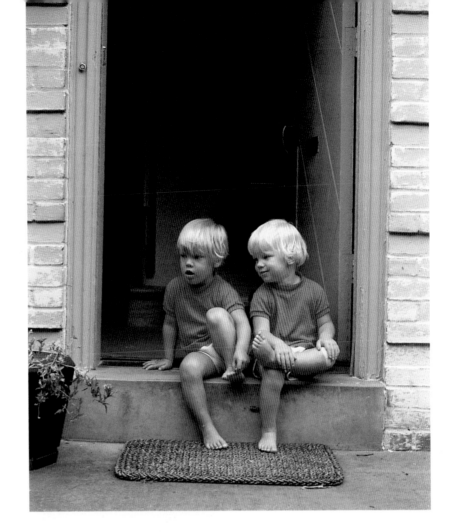

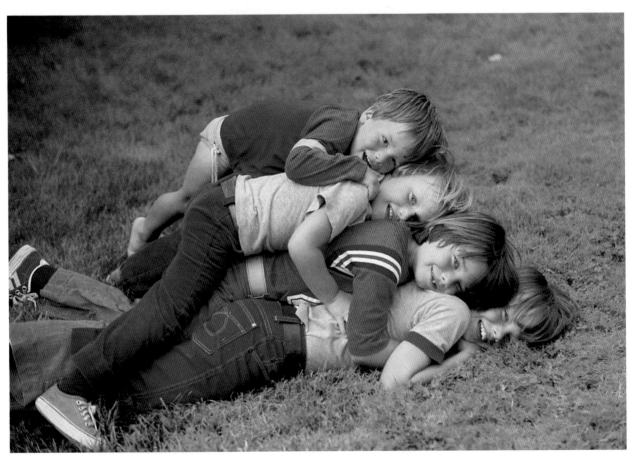

93

MORE THAN ONE

Taking a picture of a four-year-old and a baby can be tricky. Parents dream of such a picture; so do editors who like to show a perfect world. How to get it? Here, my solution was to catch Sarah as she gave the baby a quick kiss. The composition is so-so and the faces partly hidden, but at least the photograph is real.

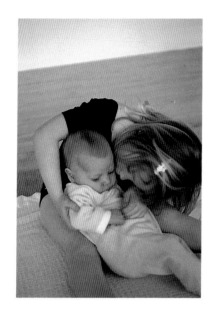

In the next picture, I asked Max to hold his baby sister. He nuzzled her and held her tight so she wouldn't fall. As a result, the baby soon began to cry. I then let them lie side by side on the bed, comfortably and safely; this made both children relaxed and happy.

Not all sister-brother shots need to be posed perfectly. Catching the children as their mother scoops them up in her arms will make a good picture, too.

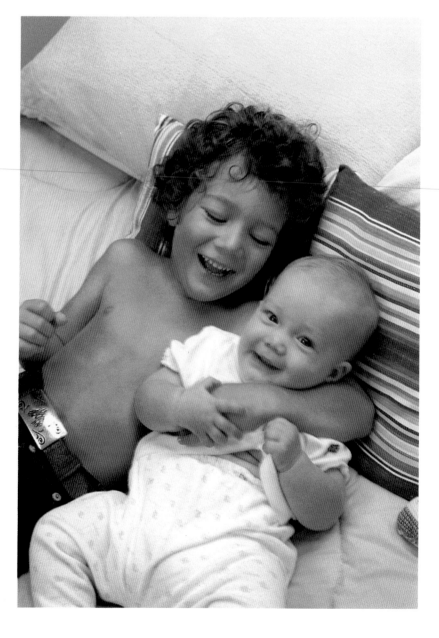

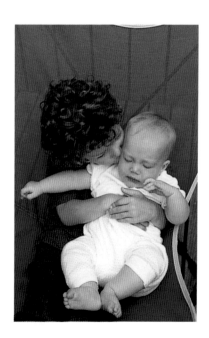

would use the older children as helpers. As the mother watched that the baby didn't fall off the bed, I gave the two older children the job of talking to the baby (for a small price), who responded right on cue with smiles. At the end of the session, the two children surrounded the baby and I got some extra shots. (Yes, it always seems that the best shots could be taken right after we pack up our cameras.) A technical note: here, two white umbrellas reflected the light from my Mecablitz 45 electronic flash with a slave, giving me f/16.

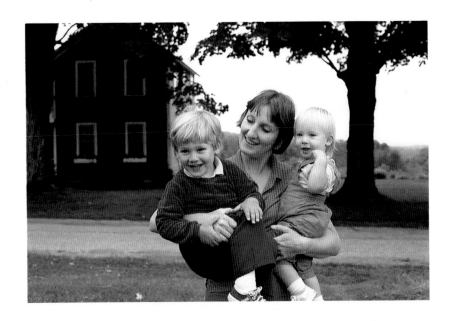

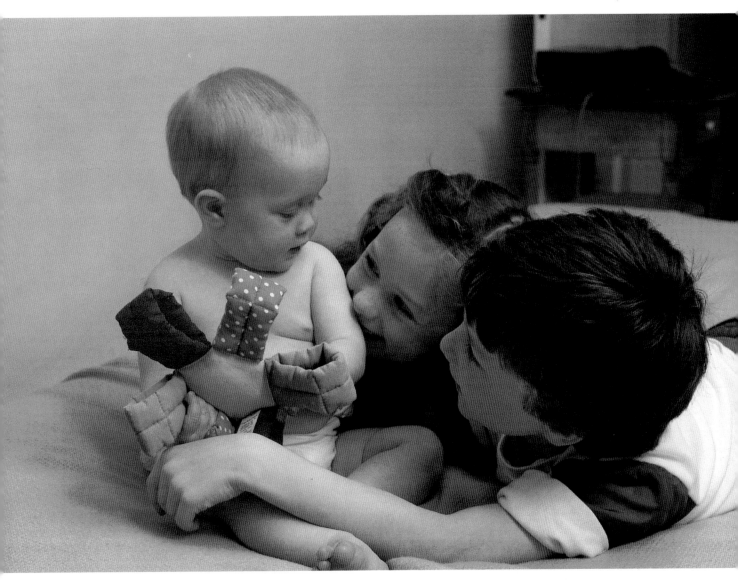

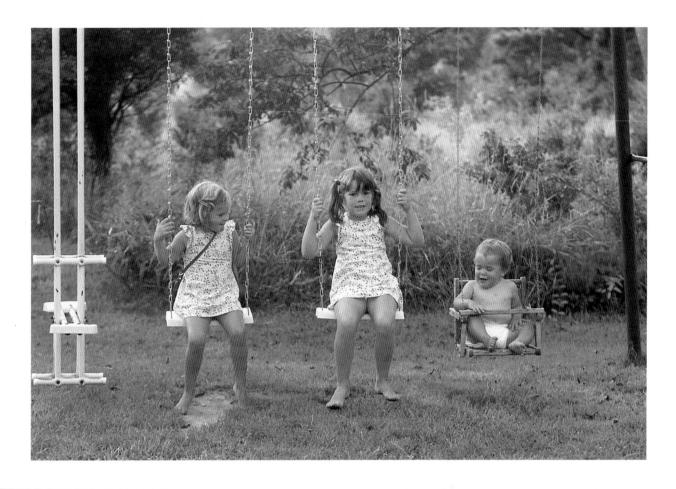

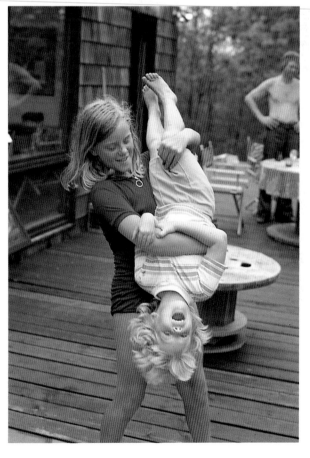

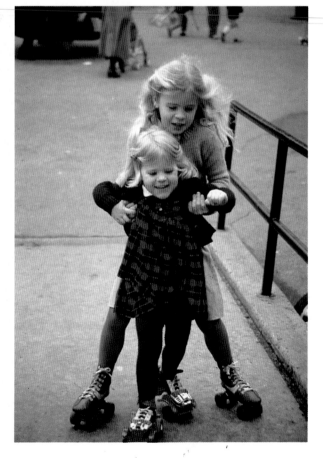

As professionals we must know how to produce pictures showing what I like to call "warmth-on-demand" and "love-on-assignment." But that doesn't mean that we must tell our subjects, the children, what we want of them.

On this assignment, the client asked for a picture of happy twins. When I heard that they liked pillow fights, I encouraged the children to go ahead and have one. They soon flopped on the bed giggling, and I grabbed the chance to show them close together. When I later asked their mother to turn the little girl around, the twins laughed even harder; this resulted in better composition.

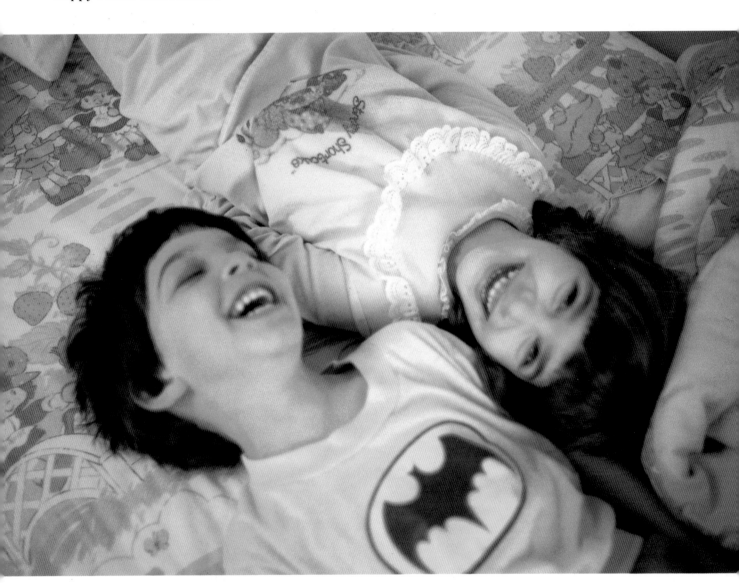

97

CHILDREN AND PARENTS

It is not easy to find families to photograph. They shouldn't be people who feel uncomfortable being photographed, nor should they be people who continually pose, worrying about how attractive they will look in the pictures.

I found "my" families in the supermarket, in school, or at parties. They may even have been private customers or people to whom a magazine once sent me on a job. But I couldn't tell that we would be able to work well together until after the first session, when some families were willing to continue their lives in my presence and others were not. As time passed, some families invited me to share their usual dinner, and if they had a spare room or a sofa, I was welcome to stay overnight. Sometimes they even took me along on trips.

These families never asked, "What do you want us to do?" They understood that I wanted to discover what *they* usually did. The parents appreciated what they got from me: flattering attention, a complete set of all black-and-white contact prints, some color transparency seconds, 10 percent of any money I made selling their pictures, a copy of any book they appeared in, and, every once in a while, a night on the town while I stayed with their children.

Some of these families have become real friends; others have moved away. Most of the children are growing up, and I often have been asked to photograph their weddings. Recently I had the pleasure of taking pictures of the second generation of children.

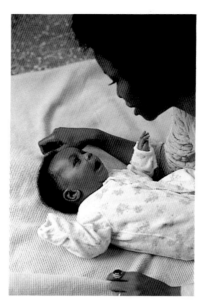

I saw little Pegge embrace her pregnant mother; the background was cluttered and obtrusive. In this instance, I interfered and asked them to move in front of the window. I bounced a small electronic flash off the ceiling to balance light coming from the windows. I bracketed one stop in both directions from my original "guesstimate"; all of the photos turned out fine. Nothing but luck—and 20 years of experience.

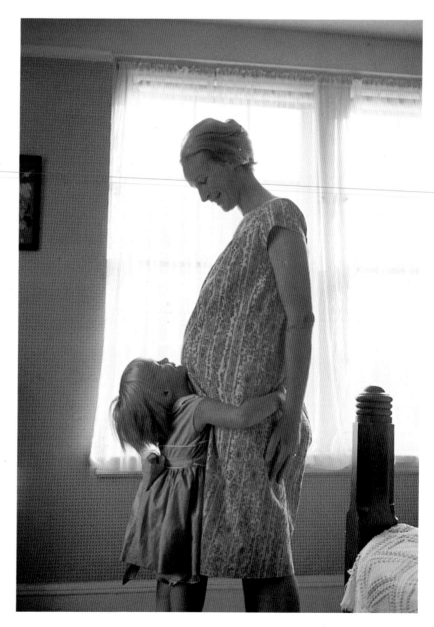

I was giving a seminar on child photography at a Long Island art association. During a question-and-answer period, a woman asked me where I find all my wonderful subjects. "I'll show you," I answered, as I turned to her neighbor, a lovely woman well along in her pregnancy. "May I photograph your baby when it is born?" The woman, whose name was Maria, was astonished for a moment and then replied, "I would be delighted. Would you also like to photograph the delivery?"

We exchanged phone numbers, and with incredible luck, I was only 20 miles from the hospital when the call came that Maria was going there to have her baby. She had, of course, arranged for my being there with her doctor and the hospital. The delivery proved to be a most relaxed and satisfying experience. The baby was born healthy and beautiful, and that set of pictures has already been printed several times. But, best of all, I have kept going back to Maria's family ever since, which also includes two older children and a father who enjoys his children. I always find something warm and exciting to photograph when I spend a morning or a day with them. Here is a shot of Maria with baby Caitlin about two weeks after her birth.

When I showed this picture at another seminar, it prompted an interesting question: "Why do so many of the women you photograph have long hair?" I was surprised to realize that this was true. The women I love to photograph are timeless mothers, vain enough to love their hair, but not vain enough to follow every whim of the trendsetters. They are women who live mostly in the countryside where natural beauty is more important than being fashionable.

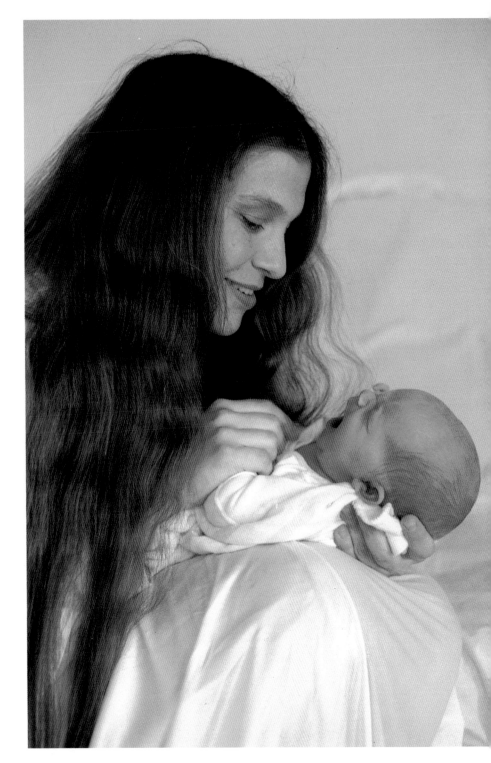

CHILDREN AND PARENTS

I really dislike posing people, but not many parents know how to hold a child for a photograph. So I compromise. Before the shot, I tell fathers and mothers, "Don't try to *see* the child. Feel it! Smell it!" Usually, the results are superior to seeing only the parent's profile as he or she lovingly gazes at the child.

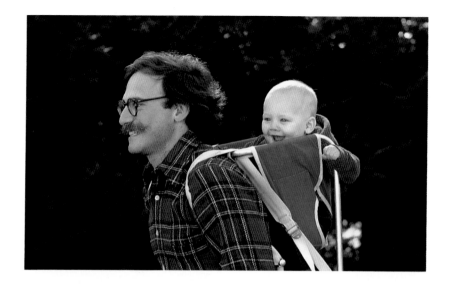

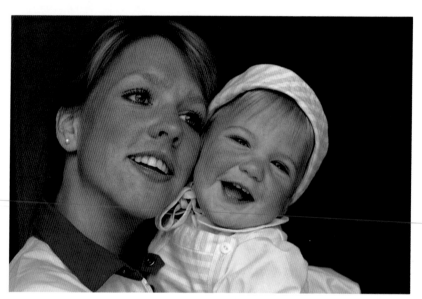

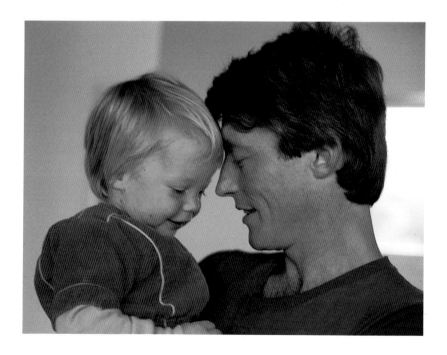

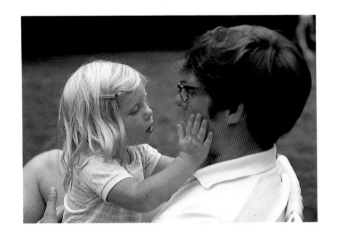

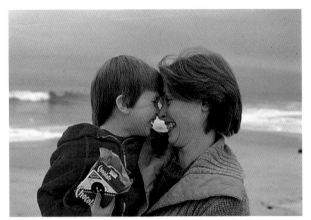

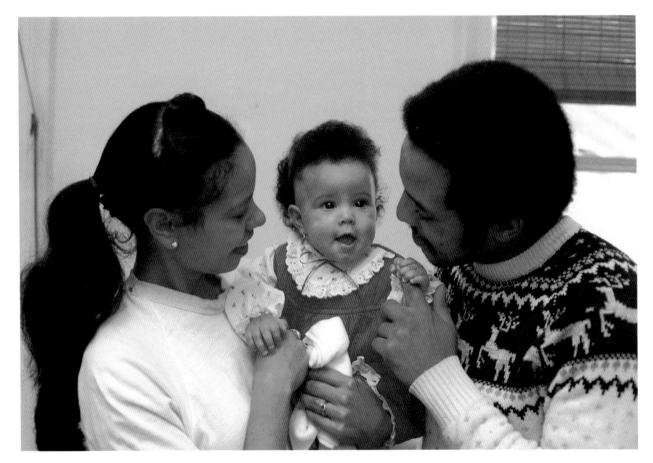

CHILDREN AND PARENTS

Here are three situations with parents and children enjoying the outdoors—in the shade. In the first shot, I needed 1/250 sec. to catch their vigorous play, so the background is slightly underexposed. I photographed the mother carrying her two small children in Vermont on an overcast day; everything is correctly exposed.

Since I was not able to find enough shade for the third picture, I asked the young parents to sit down under a tree. I took a close-up reading of the faces, locked it in, and returned to the place I wanted to shoot from. When their little boy came running toward his parents, I got a nice picture; it doesn't really matter that the grass is completely overexposed.

If you use an automatic camera for such a scene, you will have to adjust the automatic exposure lock knob, or whatever device is on your camera. Back to the manual!

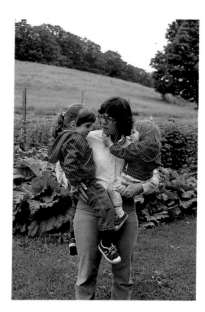

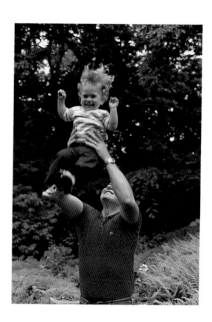

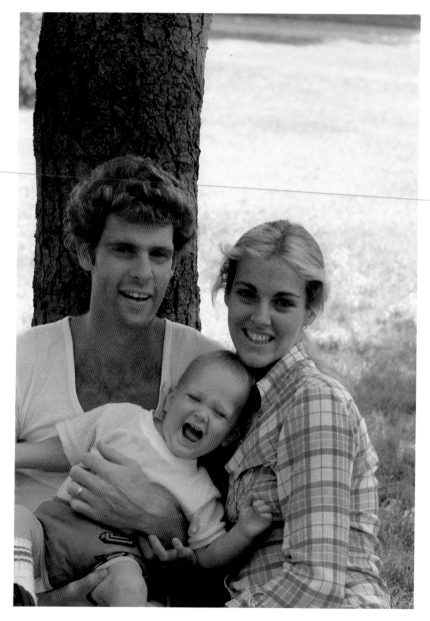

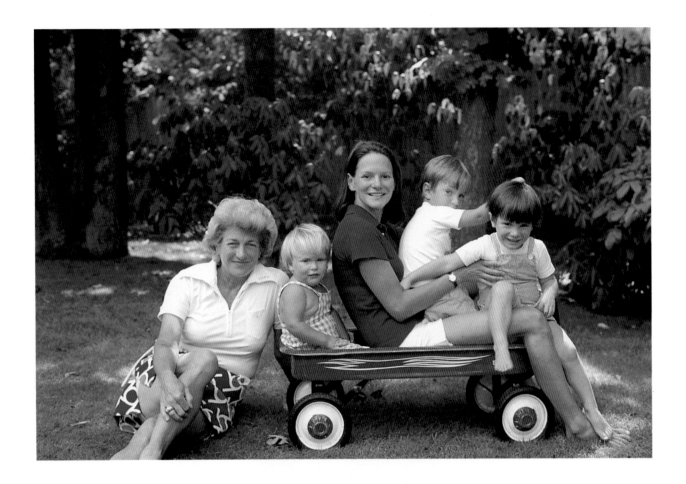

Grandparents usually prefer nicely posed, "Say cheese!" shots, but once in a while they can be persuaded to let a photographer catch them as they really are.

The first picture shows a young, handsome grandmother with her daughter and three grandchildren.

In the second picture, my husband is posing as a grandfather for an assignment. The boy quickly beat him at backgammon.

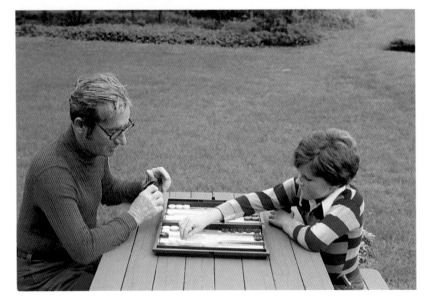

CHILDREN AND PETS

All the pets shown here belong to these children. I doubt that I could have shot such pictures if the subjects had been only superficial acquaintances. The special bond between child and pet is created by love. Animals will do certain things only with their owners; in some cases they feel close to only one member of a family. They will cuddle and sleep with that chosen person, who is not necessarily the one who feeds them.

Photographing children with pets teaches you an important lesson. You soon learn that you cannot pose an animal or force it to behave a certain way. You cannot ask it to move its head to the right or to cuddle when *you* are ready. You must set up quickly and catch what happens when it happens.

This is the best way to work—not only with pets, but also with children.

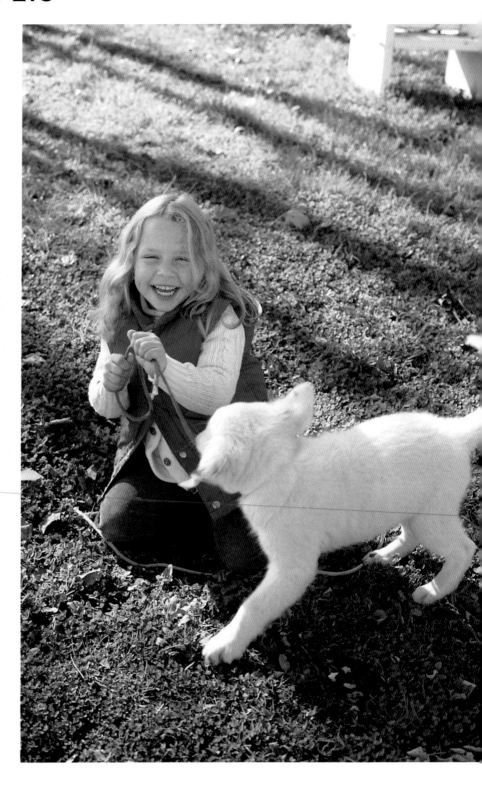

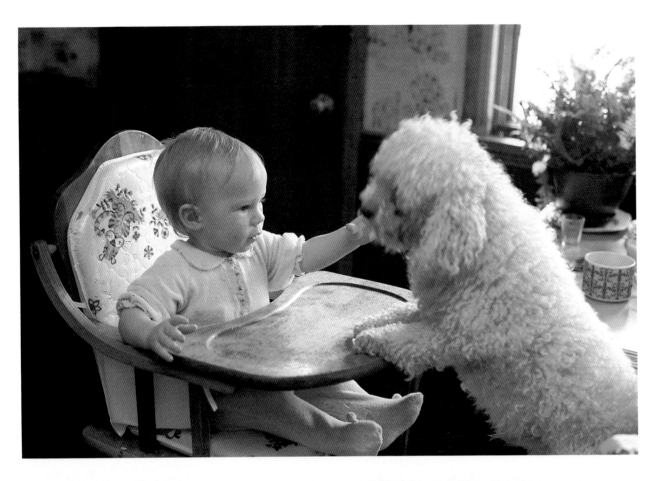

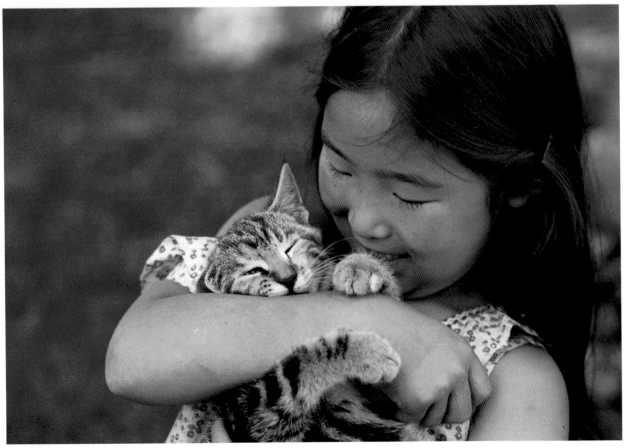

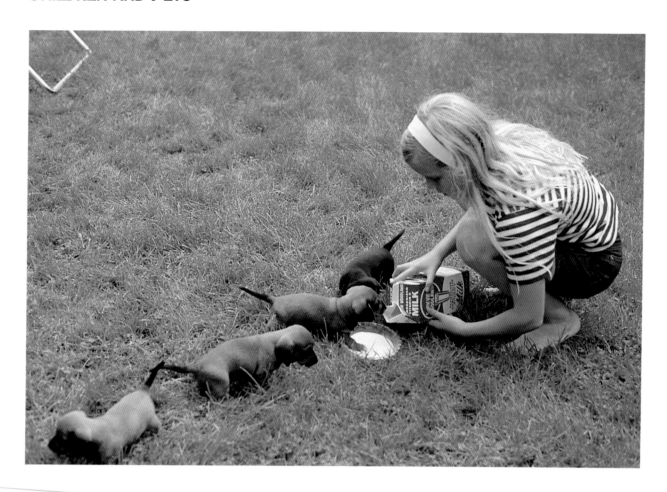

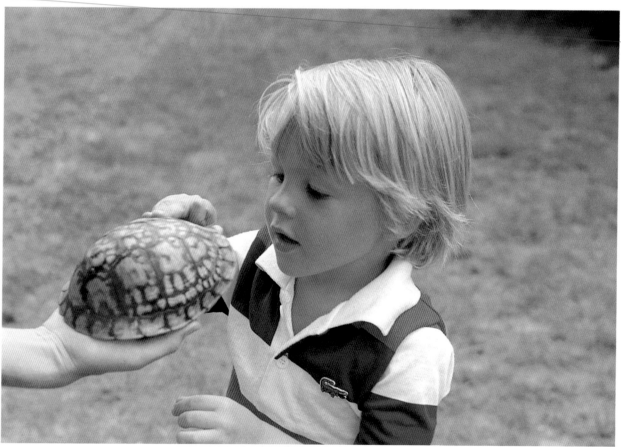

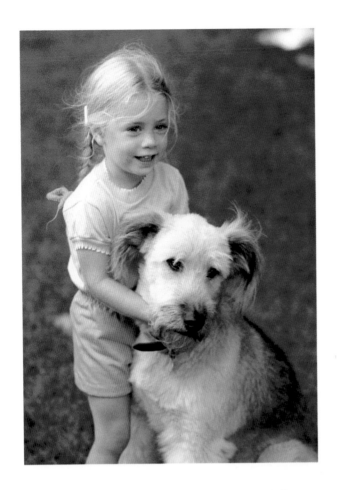

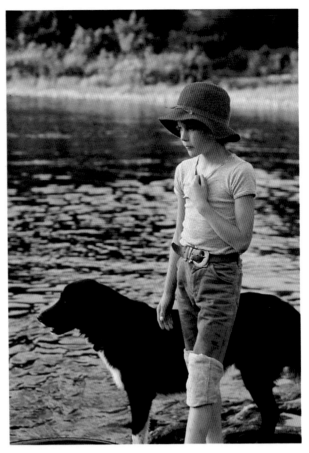

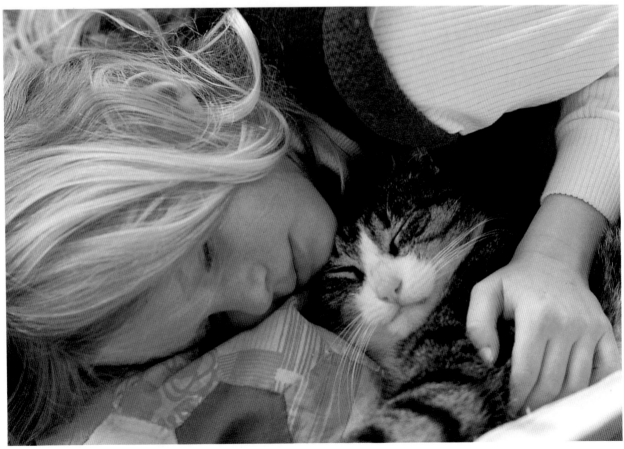

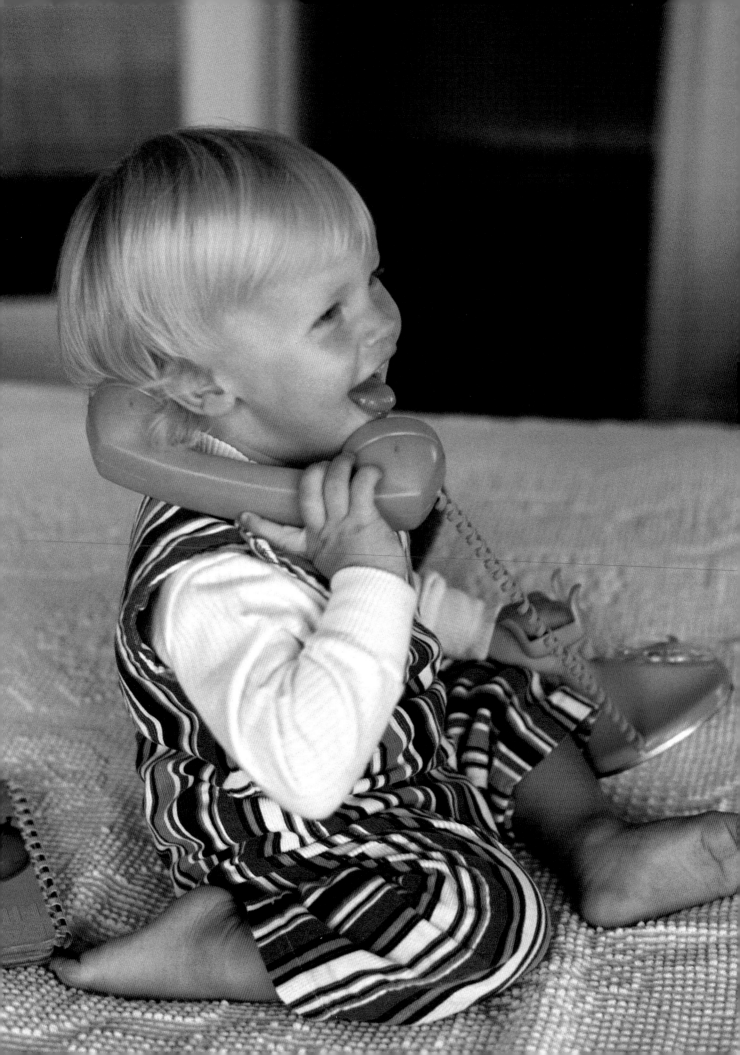

PHOTO SESSIONS CAN BE FUN

Only experience can give you the ability to think hard about exposure, sharpness, and background while at the same time tuning in on a child's mood in a relaxed way. I think you can do this only after you have learned to use your camera as automatically as you drive a car or type.

It also helps if you are aware of what the body language of children means. Reluctance to follow a suggestion can be as obvious as running away or as subtle as a pursed mouth or furrowed eyebrow. Happiness and fun are expressed by muscles pulling the whole face upward. Fear, anxiety, and sadness, on the other hand, pull these muscles downward. (Hence the expressions of being in an "up" or "down" mood.)

Should this subject interest you, my book, *The Body Language of Children* (New York: W. W. Norton, 1978), could prove of value to you.

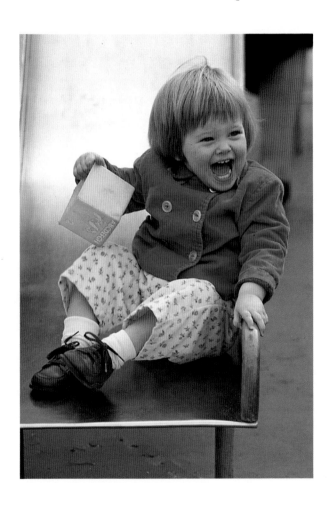
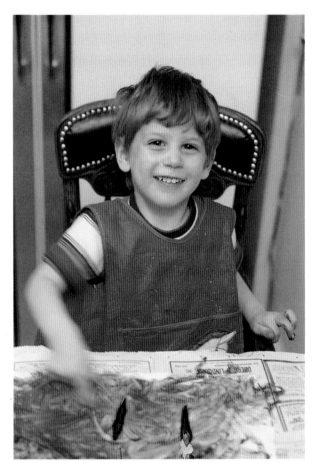

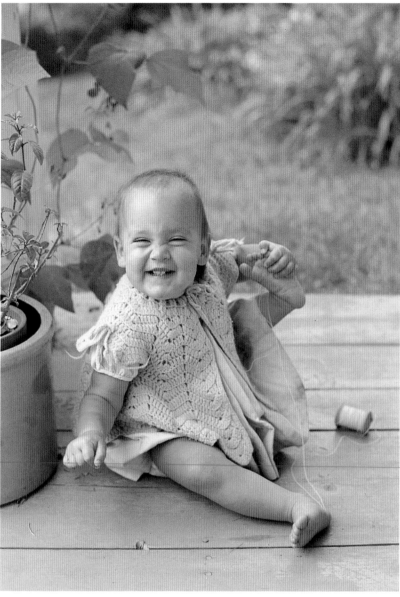

What else can you do to make sure that the photo session is fun for the children? I said earlier that I don't make friends with them. But I did not say that I resist if one of the little charmers wants to make friends with me. Occasionally I also make a funny face or balance something on

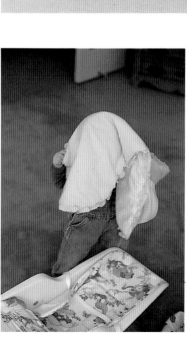

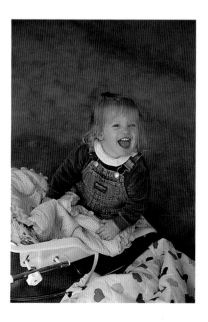

my head if I see that the child enjoys such games. As you can see in the first picture, I had been flirting with little Sarah.

In the second and third pictures, the child did the wooing, initiating the fun of playing peekaboo. Let me be serious for a moment: the game of peekaboo produces hysterical happiness because at this age the child is learning that people who seem lost while they cover their head reappear. This is an important discovery for a child and a very useful tool for the photographer.

Giant bubbles are fun and games for a child, but give the photographer a headache. Will the bubbles stand out against the background? Are they moving too fast? Have I hit the right exposure for a scene with such contrasts? Luckily, sometimes everything works.

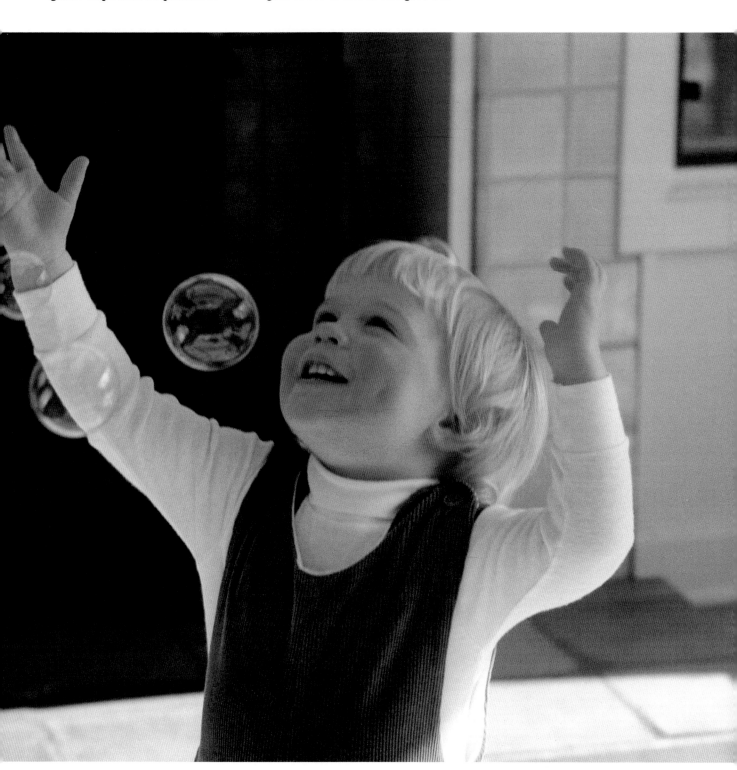

CHILDREN'S CHOICES

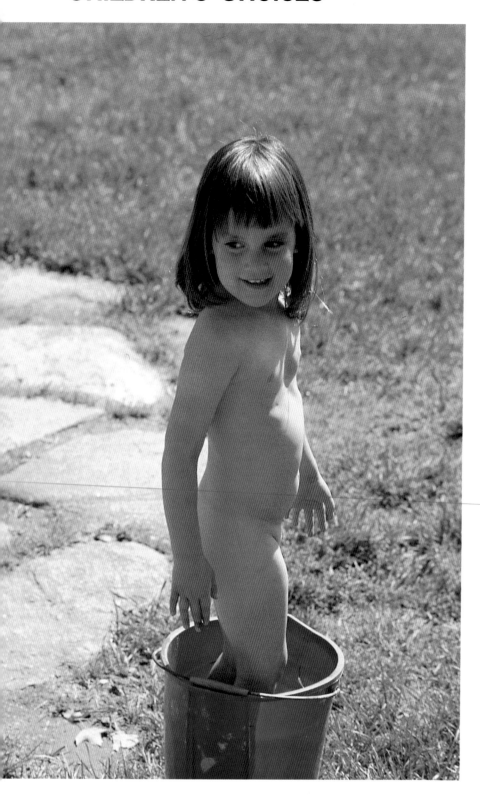

One of my favorite ways to spark up a sitting that is going badly is to ask the children, "How would *you* like to be photographed?" Some children think that I am joking and that I won't actually take a picture of them standing in a pail of water or hanging upside down from a swing. Then when I do, they sparkle and giggle and have a really good time.

In the shots in this section, one girl painted her face, and another dressed up in her mother's old clothes. Two other little girls wanted to wear masks. The future Reggie Jackson wanted only to be photographed playing baseball.

Children teach us photographers something. They show us that our imagination is feeble, that they can think of more interesting things than we can. So why tell them how to sit, what to do, or what to wear when their inventiveness and playfulness are superior to ours?

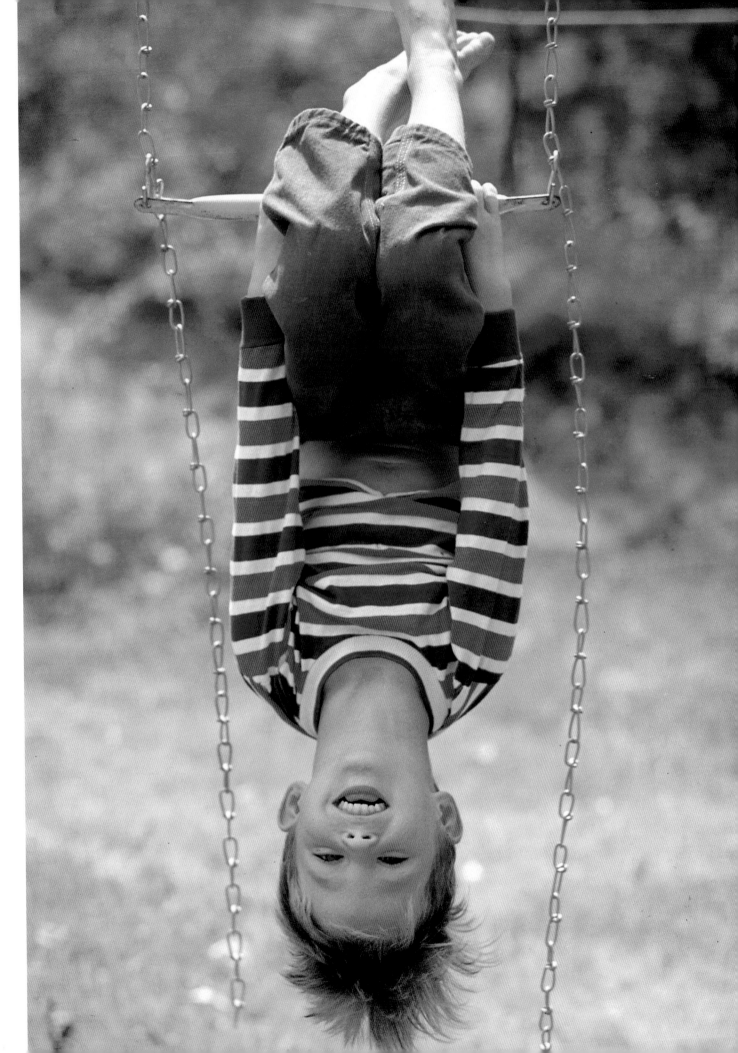

CHILDREN'S CHOICES

I for one have learned to respect my subjects' contributions to the photographic session. I allow the children to guide me if they want to; they love to feel that they are in charge. And if they suggest climbing up a tree, I don't worry. When they come down, I can probably get them to wear their fancy clothes for a few minutes. Fair is fair. And Grandma and Grandpa will be happy with the photographs, too.

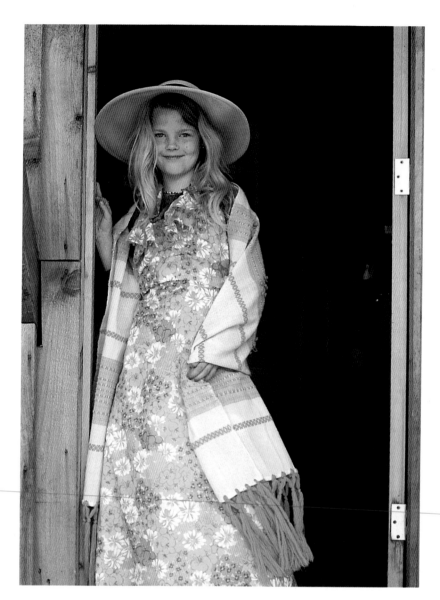

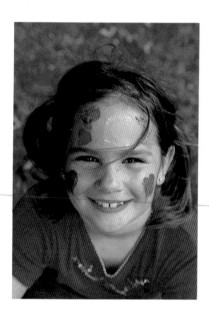

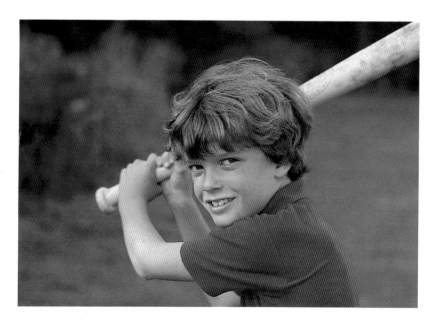

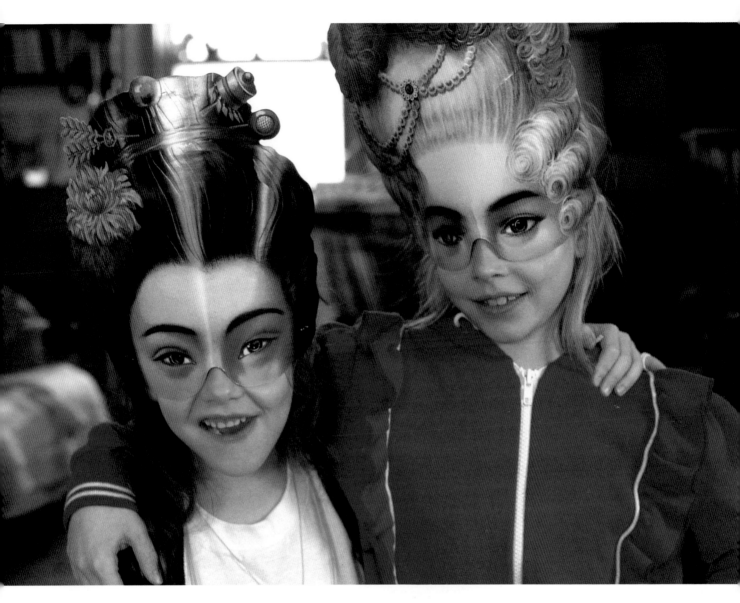

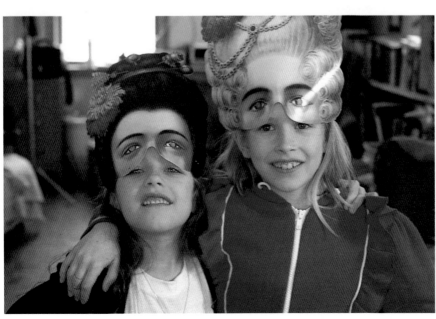

CHILDREN AT PLAY

Play is children's work. Knowing this, we photographers respect it and never intrude on a fantasy or destroy a child's castle simply because, after all, it is just play.

It is through play that children learn, come to understand the difference between make-believe and reality, and test their talents and skills.

I consider it part of my job to record their progress, marvel at their imagination, and spread the cause of understanding children.

Here is a checklist of what to and what not to do when photographing children at play.

DO

- Wear shoes that allow you to move about silently
- Carry only one or at the most two cameras at a time
- Keep your extra film in a pouch on your belt
- Examine your shots from all angles: right and left, down low and high up

DON'T

- Don't use flash unless absolutely necessary; the sudden light will distract your subjects
- Don't comment on their efforts when they paint or sculpt; they are not working in order to get praise or criticism

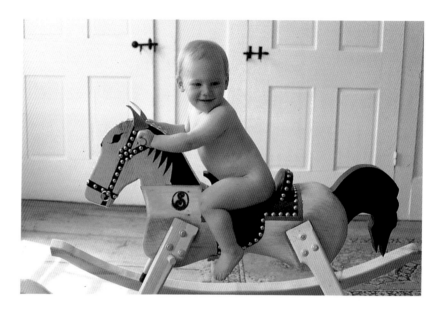

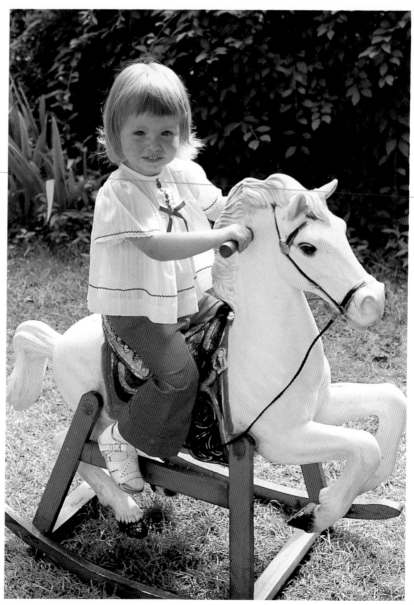

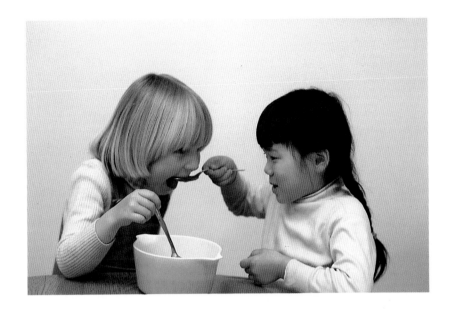

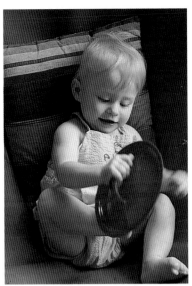

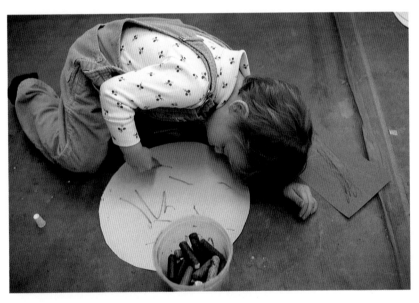

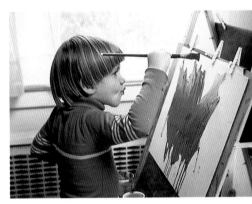

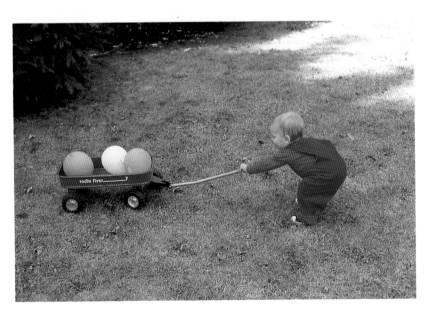

CHILDREN AT PLAY

I love music, dancing, singing games, and learning to play instruments. So whenever I notice a recorder or a trumpet in a child's room, I ask him or her to play for me. Sometimes we end up singing harmony to "Twinkle, Twinkle, Little Star" or "Old MacDonald Had a Farm."

I once did a brochure for the Third Street Settlement Music School, and I was in seventh heaven. The children didn't move much while playing, so I was able to shoot with available light most of the time. I was pleased that hardly anyone noticed my presence.

You will be rewarded with good photographs if you allow children to get really engrossed in their play.

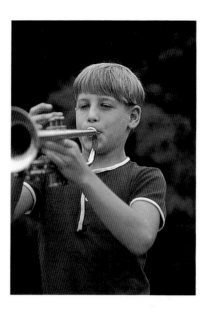

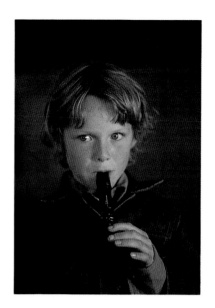

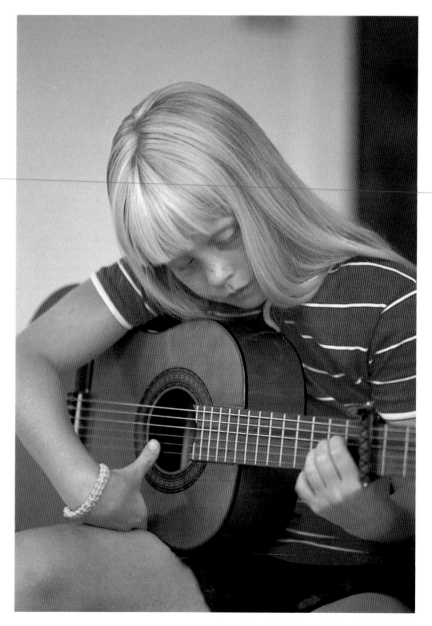

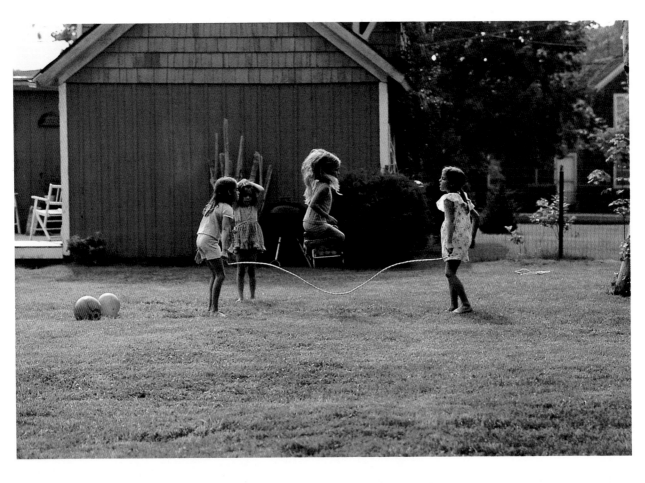

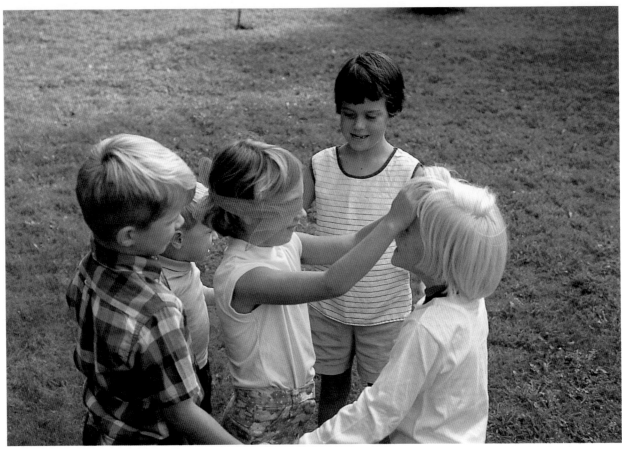

OFF TO SCHOOL

I was allowed to photograph in a school for the first time when one of the parents I knew happened to be the head of the local PTA. After mentioning my interest in following her four-year-old child around school, she volunteered to talk to the principal. I then went on an interview, mostly to explain what I wanted to do with the pictures. Luckily, I had already been published in a textbook so my credibility was quickly established. I said that I would give the school any picture it wanted for brochures or fund raising.

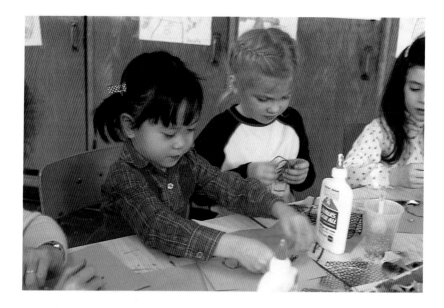

"But what if a parent objects?" the principal asked. I promised that, except for textbook use, I would seek permission from the parents themselves. To facilitate this, I then asked for a list of the students' names. (Later I identified as many of the children as I could while I still remembered who each one was. Once again, my numbering system came in handy.)

While talking with the principal, I emphasized that I would be quiet, use no flash, and not fuss over some children more than others. This was the start of some very satisfying school sessions.

In one school (with an enrollment of about 500), I ventured to photograph every child and then let the school sell the photographs to the parents. They made over $4,000 for their building fund (I only asked for my lowest day rate), and I later sold a story on the idea, illustrated with the best pictures, to *Popular Photography*.

Try this in local schools. Make sure that you have enough volunteers to mail out contact prints, ask for orders, and then mail out the enlargements. Otherwise, you will spend too much time on all the arrangements, even if the school is willing to pay your minimum day rate.

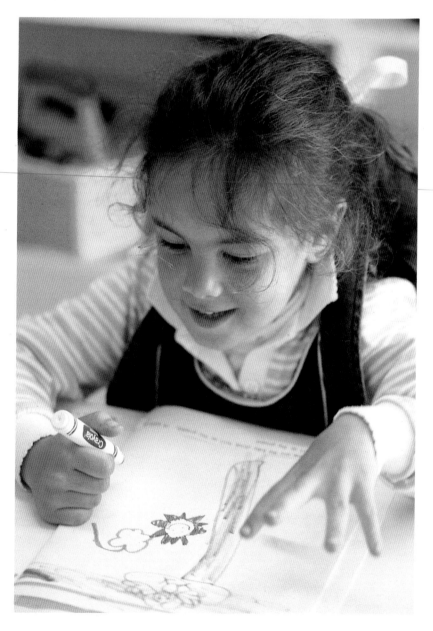

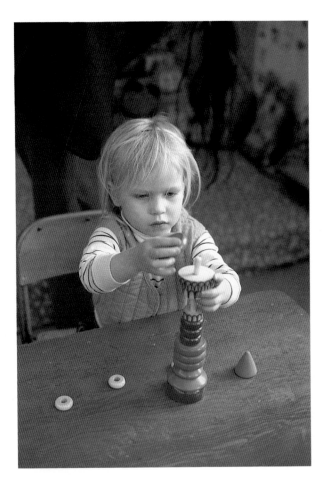

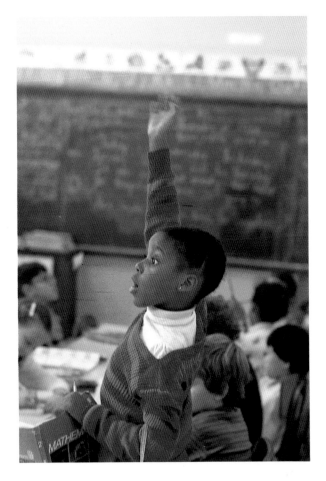

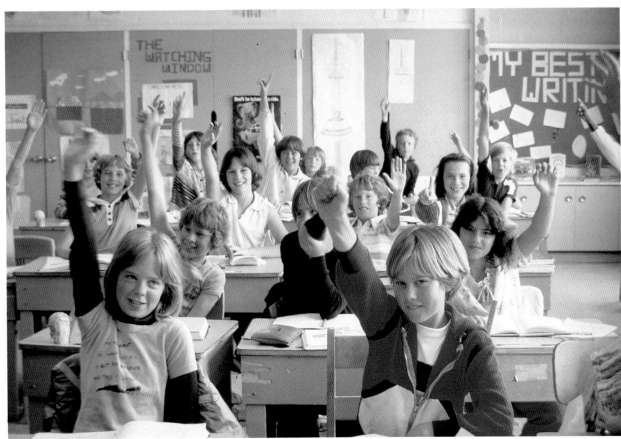

Schoolrooms are predominantly light, airy places where taking pictures is a pleasure. But in some older schools walls are painted vibrant, strong colors, so be careful not to let reflections affect your photographs.

While shooting, I sometimes want to move closer to a child, but I don't want to disrupt the teaching. Luckily, few schools still have children sit in rows all facing the same way, so it is easier for me to move around. Occasionally I sit in an empty desk and shoot from there.

Be prepared for all kinds of reactions from students—sometimes from teachers, too. Naturally, I always explain my presence to the teacher, and, if he or she gives me permission, I address the class as well. I quiet their guesses that they "will be in the paper" and tell them that if I can arrange it, they will eventually see their pictures. I also ask that they go on with their work since I am not photographing *them*, but what they are doing.

I find being in a classroom fascinating. Reliving this time is only one of the rewards of photographing children. I also get to share such other memorable experiences as births, tonsillectomies, broken legs, athletic triumphs and defeats, first haircuts, and last days in summer camp.

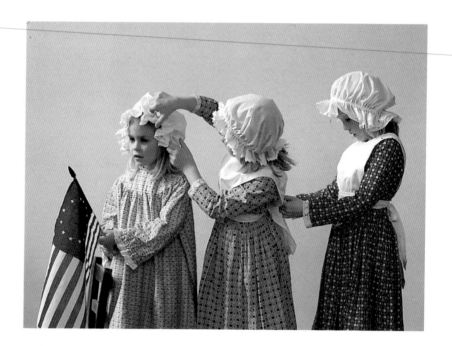

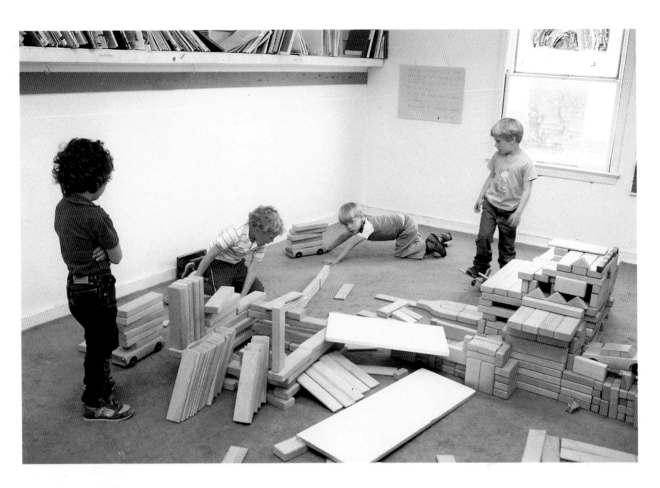

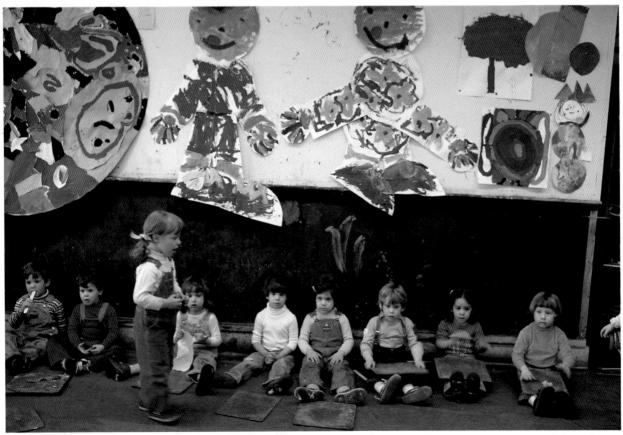

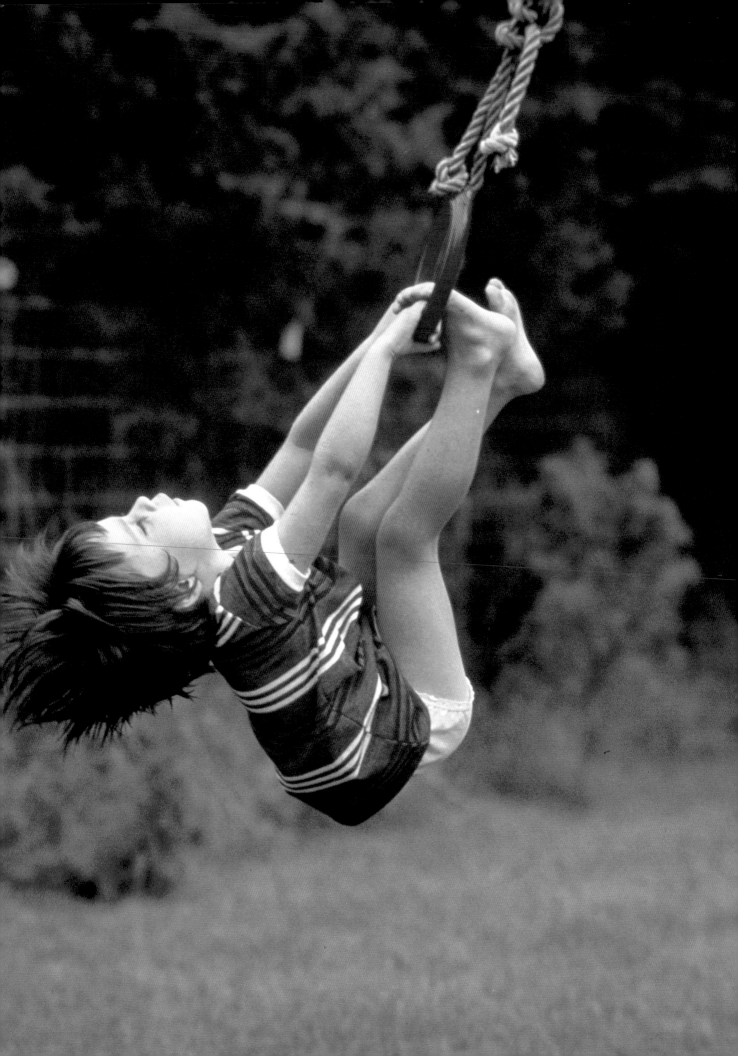

When it comes to children, the importance of running, jumping, hitting a ball, or swinging from a tree limb cannot be overestimated. More than their physical health is at stake: I have always been a believer in the sound mind/sound body idea.

It is also wonderful for them to grow up knowing how to move on the ice or snow properly, hit a ball easily, and be courageous and self-confident.

Children feel good showing off their skills in front of the camera. And they love to collect pictures of their sports heroes. Here the unique quality of a still photo shows up. The time spent watching a sports idol in real life or on television passes quickly. But the poster, clipping, or enlargement that hangs on the wall and that the child greets upon awakening has a more lasting impression and will play a greater role in the child's life.

When photographing children's sports activities, we must react quickly. It also helps if we know something about the game or sport the children are engaged in, to anticipate the direction of the ball or keep out of the way.

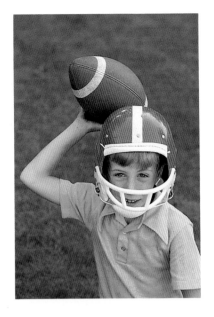

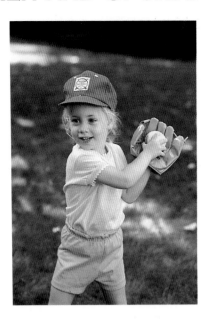

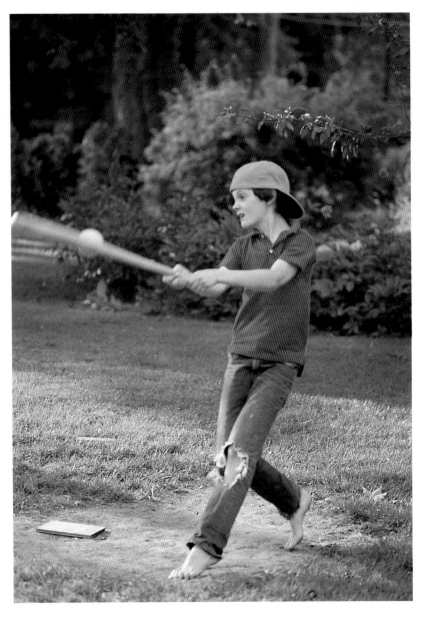

CHILDREN AND SPORTS

Two new steps in camera design have made covering sports easier. First, the shutter speed at which an electronic flash can be synchronized with the general exposure has been changed from a minimum of 1/60 sec. to an even shorter 1/250 sec. This means that you can lighten the shaded side of the subjects (shooting against the light, for instance) while being sure that fast movements will not be blurred. More and more cameras are following Nikon and Minolta's lead in this significant improvement in photographing fast action.

The other change is just as helpful: there are now cameras that follow the moving subject and focus themselves on it automatically.

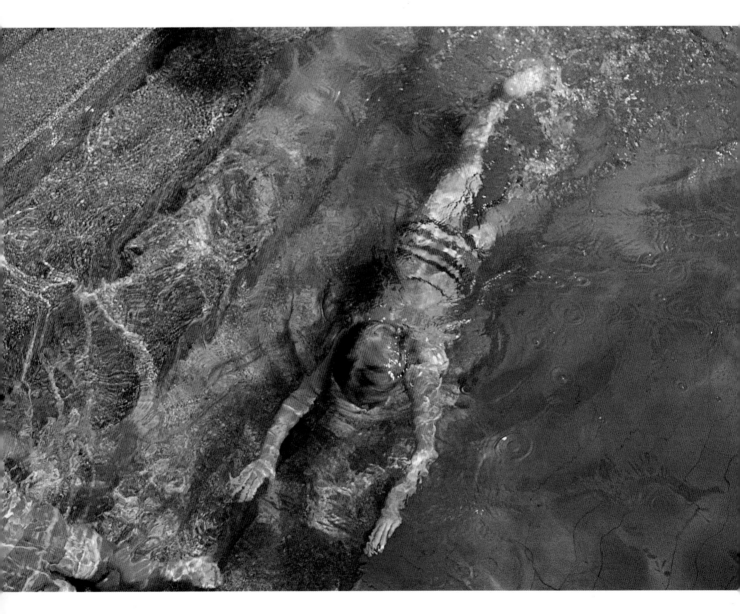

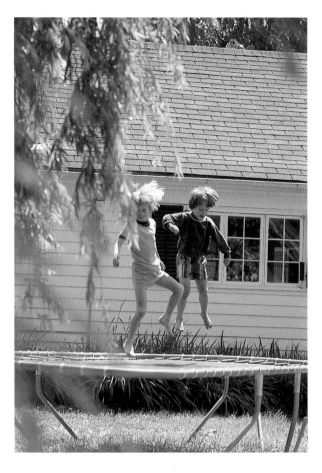

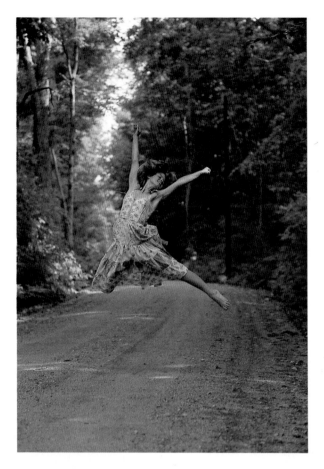

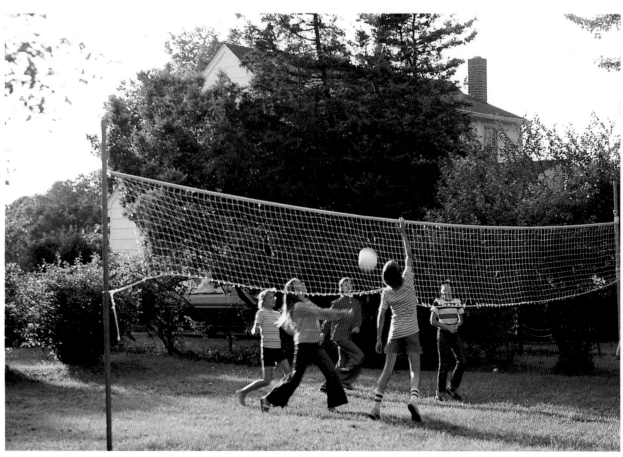

SPECIAL OCCASIONS

I love to get holiday cards and I also like to make them. My favorite is this photo of a little girl with her big dog, walking in the snow under an overcast sky. At first I worried that there was no detail in the snow; but a clean white is better than a bluish cast that can be the result of a clear blue sky.

The problem with Christmas and Hanukkah cards is that you have to make them a year ahead of time, or, at least, that you have to shoot enough winter scenes to pick from the following year.

I keep a few of my small mounted photographs to send as get well or congratulations cards throughout the year. Maybe one day I will use the picture of this delightful "bunny" I photographed during an Easter egg hunt.

And, as a last resort, you can always fake a holiday card. My friend Betty called me one day in September, excited that her whole family would soon be visiting from near and far. Could we shoot a Christmas card? Well, between the two of us, I think we succeeded. We dragged some benches in front of pine trees, put a freshly made wreath on the tree, and dressed everyone in festive colors. I made sure that I took the photographs in the very early evening, just after the sun went down—and bingo! a nice Christmas card.

One of the reasons so many holiday pictures turn out so well is that everyone is too busy to worry about posing. It is also an occasion of family togetherness.

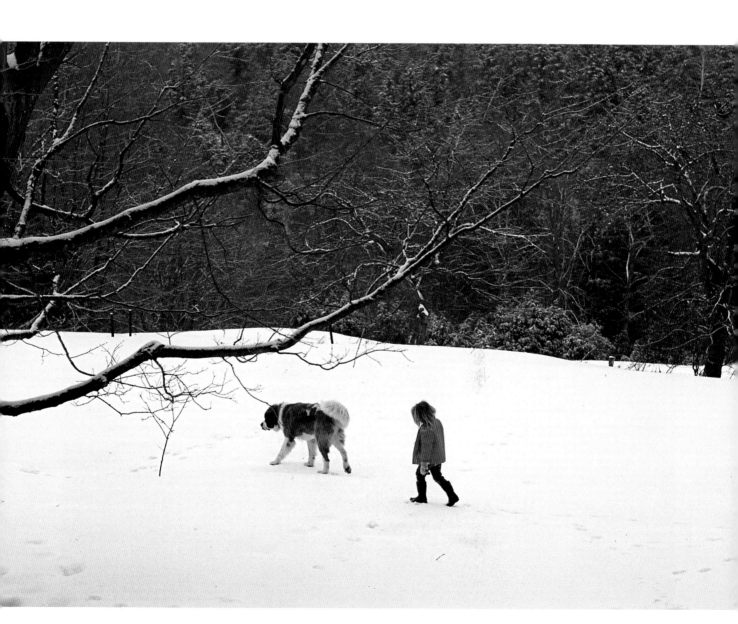

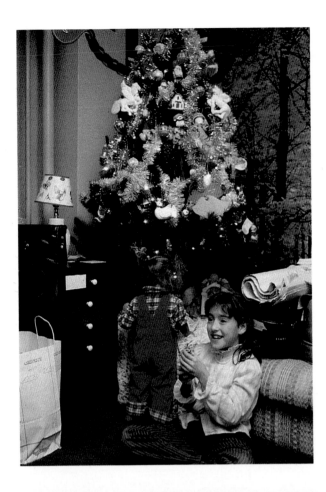

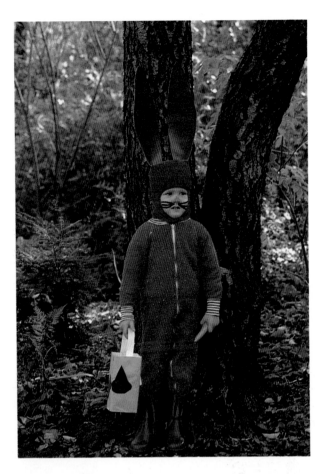

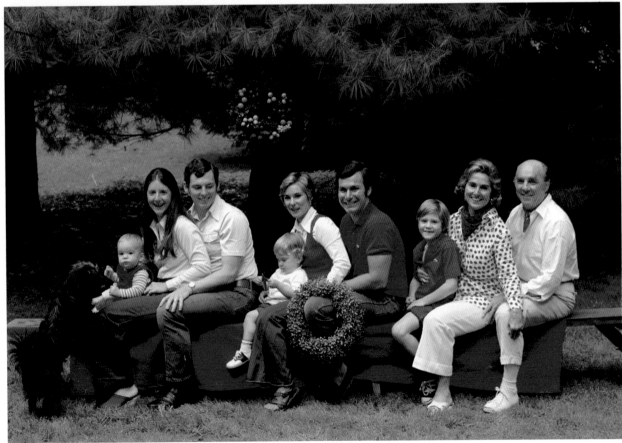

Special Occasions

Last Halloween, I decided to try out my new Minolta 320 automatic electronic flash, which measures the flash duration needed for each picture. I was very doubtful. How could such a small unit know what to do?

The box had a little green light that stayed on for a few seconds every time it approved the *f*-stop I had set.

After more than 30 years in photography, I am used to that terrifying moment when my color film is ready at the lab. But I behaved like a novice when I saw these transparencies. They were just too good to be true.

I prefer to photograph birthdays using tungsten-balanced film with photofloods, unless there is a lot of daylight in the room. With my method, the lights are on all the time and the candles are more likely to show well. (But before you try this system, please reread the section on tungsten lights.)

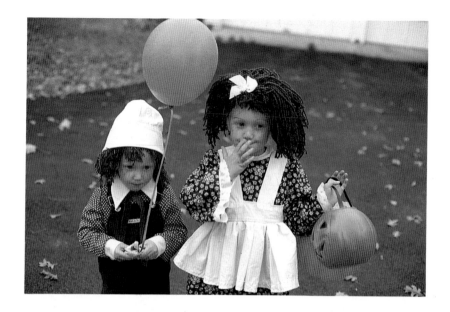

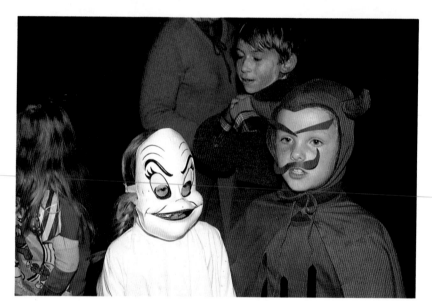

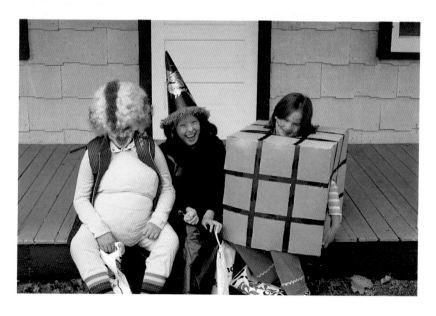

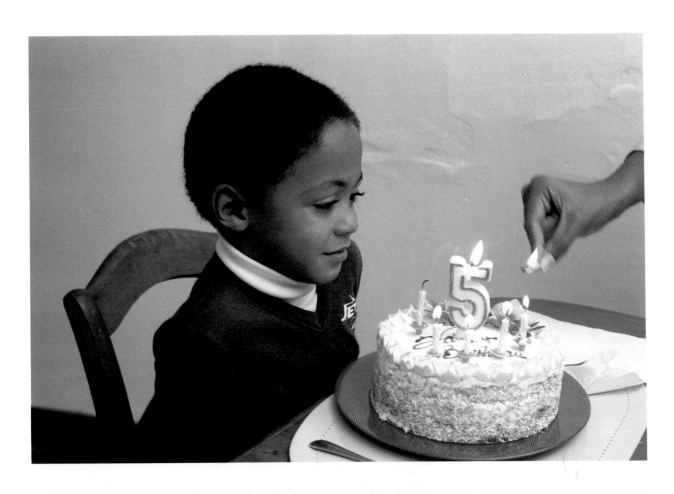

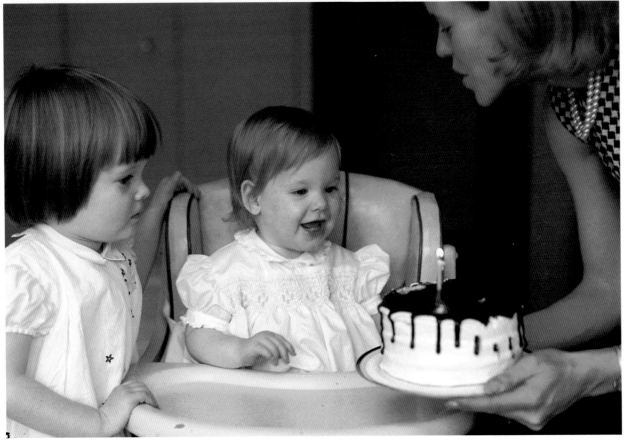

Unusual Expressions: Not for the Reject Pile

I have to admit that I prefer a funny, even outrageous expression on a child's face to a well-bred, polite smile any time. But I hope that my enthusiasm about the photographs in this chapter stems not from my hobby of collecting oddities, but from my realization that children are complex human beings with a variety of complicated feelings, which are reflected in their unusual expressions.

I think it's wonderful when parents enjoy such pictures as much as I do. This means that they accept all of their children's moods and feelings; it also shows that they understand and value their children's body language.

As for how to create your own collection of unusual expressions, I can only suggest once again that you free yourself from directing your subjects, learn a simple way to handle your equipment, and become aware of what is happening before your eyes.

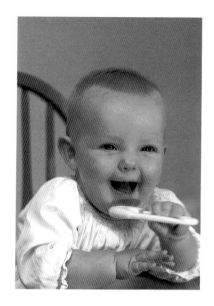

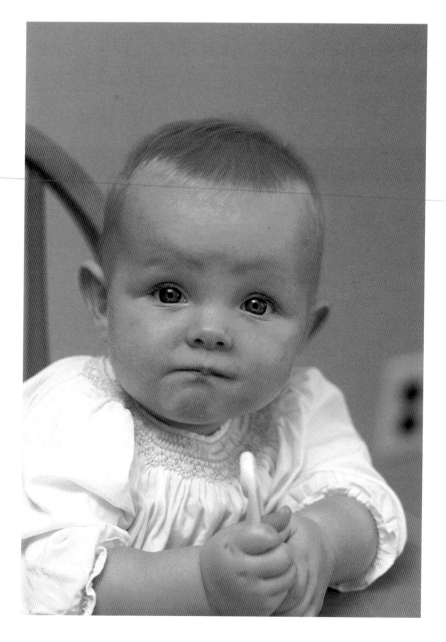

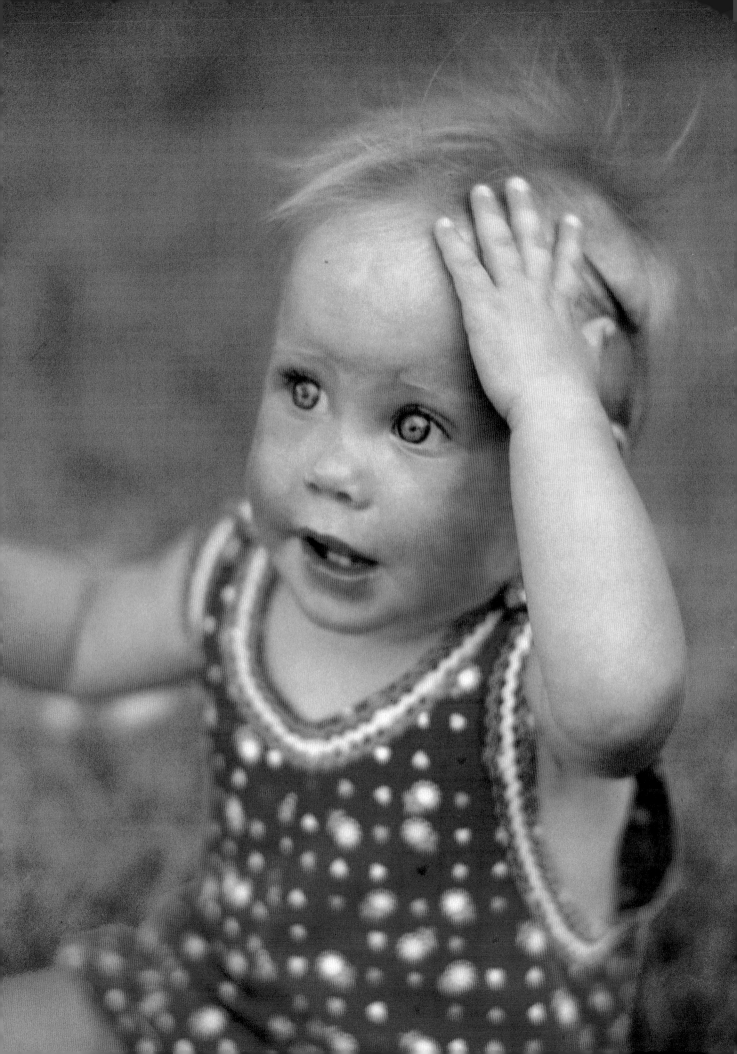

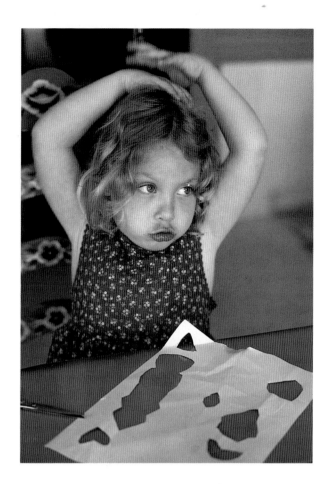

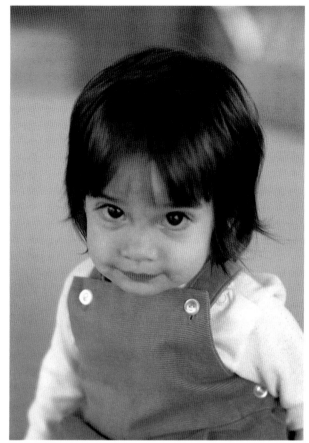

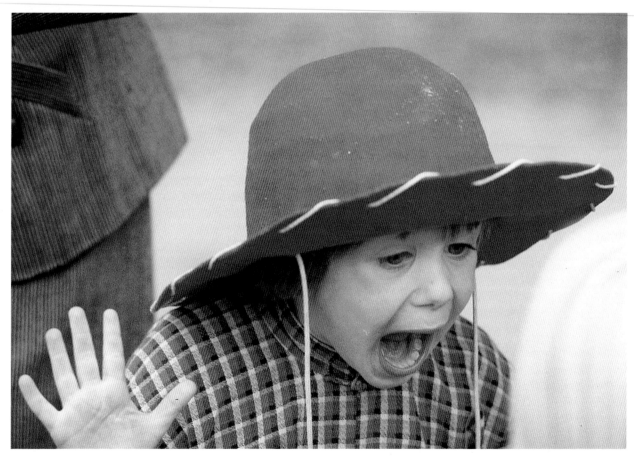

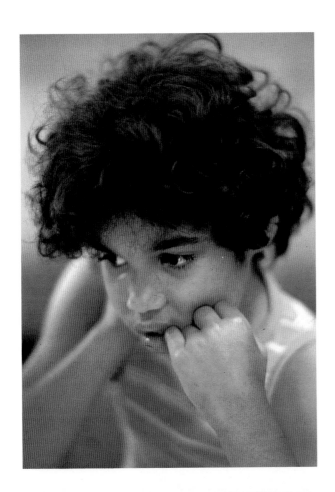

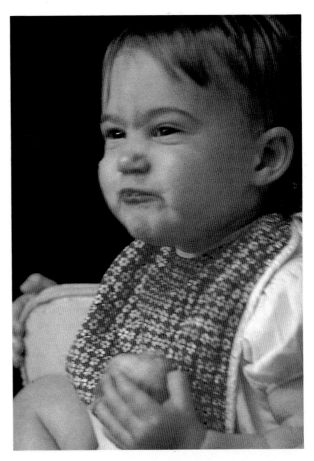

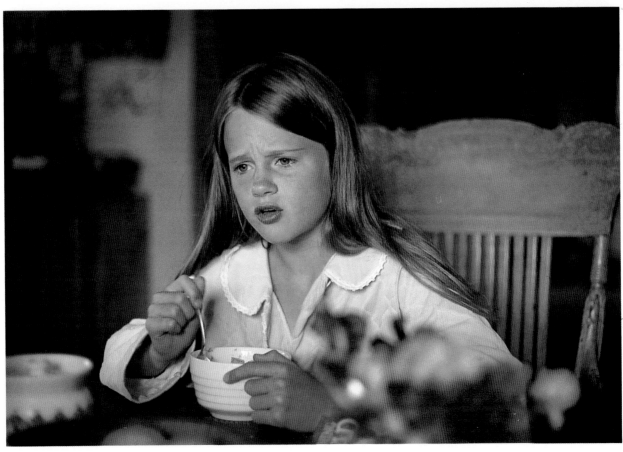

VACATIONS TO REMEMBER

I enjoy every aspect of being a photographer. I like recording the lives of children; hunting for subjects when I get an assignment or have an idea for a picture story; editing; writing captions and text; and even doing the darkroom work when I am preparing a book or an exhibition. I also like to do my own filing. This work reminds me of all the thousands of photographs I've taken. Because of this familiarity with my work, I am able to put together books and articles frequently. The latest article (and exhibit as well) is called "Juxtapositions"; it consists of pairs of my photographs arranged by design, time lapse, or content.

I have only one reservation about the life of a photographer: you get no true vacation—ever. If you go to the beach without your camera, some trick of the light may transform a well-known scene into something unusual, or an elf of a child may keep digging her toes into the water in a most charming way.

As for travelling, it's hard just to enjoy the scenery and not start a new "job." And how much equipment and film should you carry? I pack about 10 rolls of my two favorite films into an insulated bag for a day's shooting and add my smallest electronic flash for a fill-in. Gone are the days when I loaded nearly everything I owned into the trunk of my car so anything I could possibly need was at my fingertips. (My trunk has been robbed twice; I would be foolhardy ever to leave anything of value in it again, even for a short time.)

But enough of my complaints. Let's look at the vacation pictures I have taken of my friends and amateur models or on assignments. As you can see, I am always eager to portray not only a landscape, but also the moods and feelings of the people enjoying it.

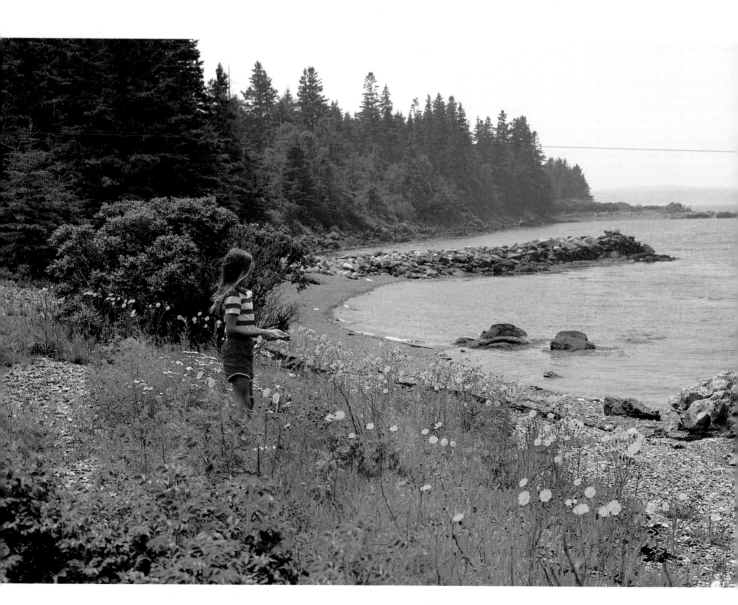

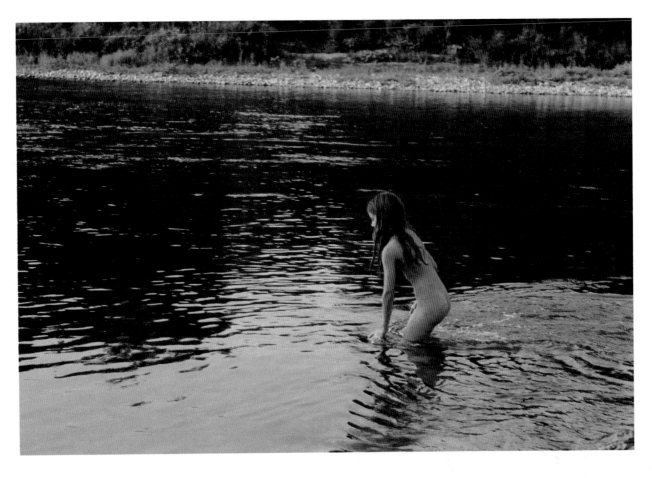

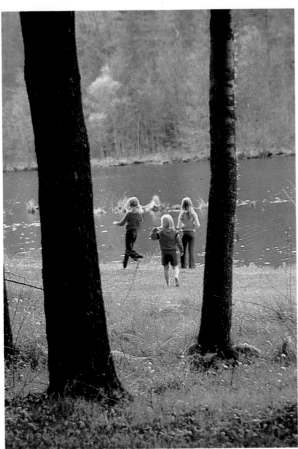

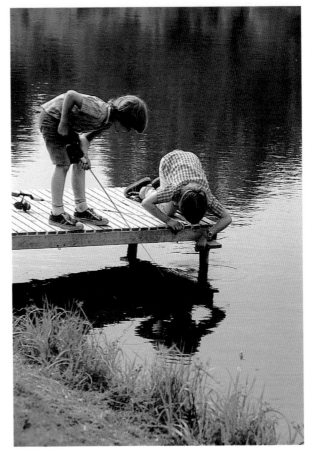

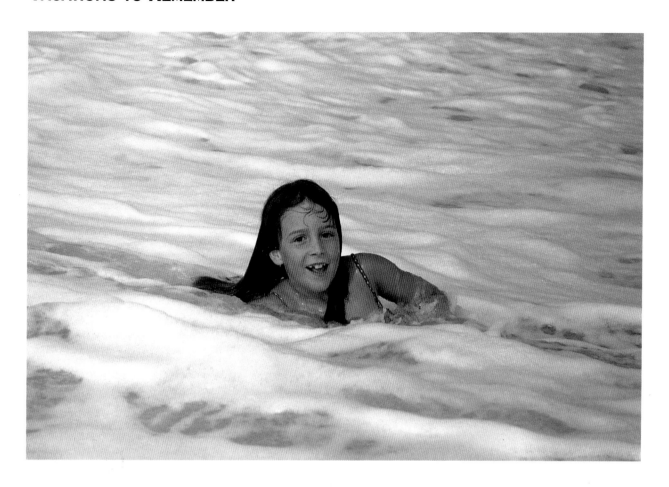

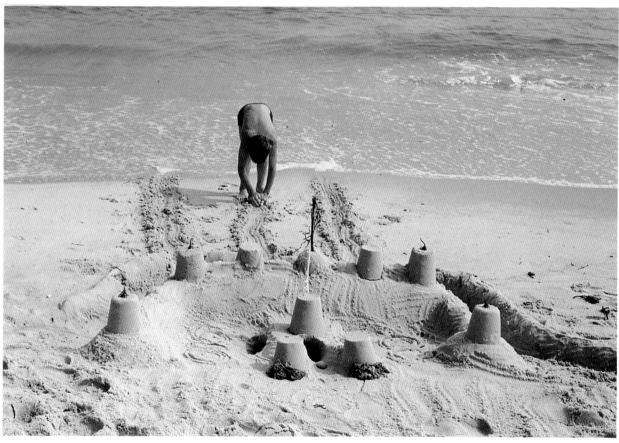

Because I like to photograph in overcast weather, I always have warming filters mounted on my lenses. They alleviate the bluish cast of pictures taken in the shade or on an overcast day.

The last two photographs show you the difference between snow photographed when it is overcast and when the sun is out. The overcast sky removes all detail from the snow, which then becomes simply a lovely background for the child's portrait. When the sun is out, the snow is full of detail and thus attracts attention to itself.

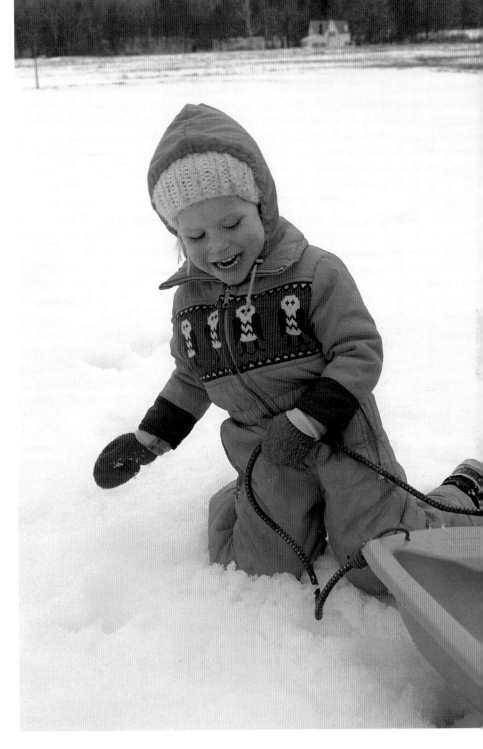

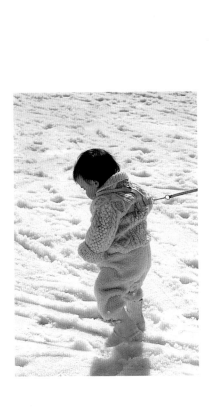

A SEQUENCE: THE TWO BALLOONS

Sequences are a still photographer's movies.

A lucky combination of candid shooting and quick orchestration produced this sequence. I had given Nat a red balloon and started taking pictures while he blew it up. I didn't notice that his older brother had come over when all of a sudden—whoosh!—the balloon was gone. Billy had punctured it with a pin. My impulse to give Nat another balloon was originally meant only to console him, but I soon saw the possibilities in rounding out this little drama by asking Nat's father to blow up the blue balloon and give it to Nat.

The next day, when I saw my developed transparencies, I found that I had to go back to repeat one picture. Guess which one! The pin was completely invisible in the first pictures of Billy's hand, which I had posed. I had to supply a much larger pin so that it would be clearly visible as it was about to puncture the red balloon.

Naturally, this work would not have been interesting without Nat's wonderfully sensitive, changing expressions or his parents' enthusiasm as they entered into the spirit of our little improvisation.

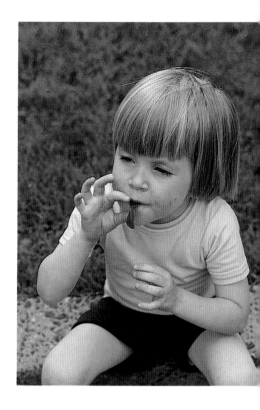

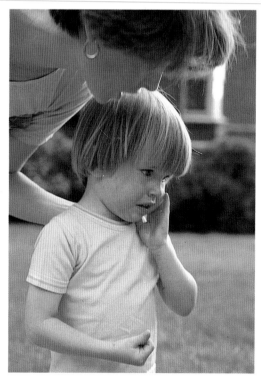

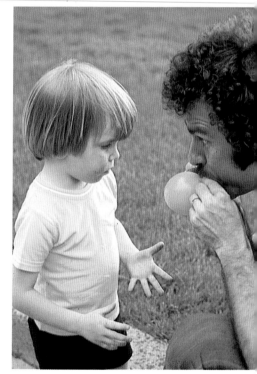

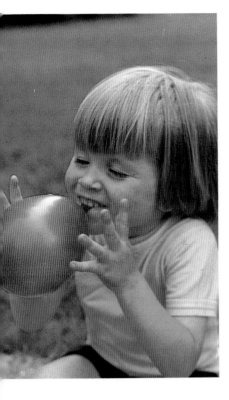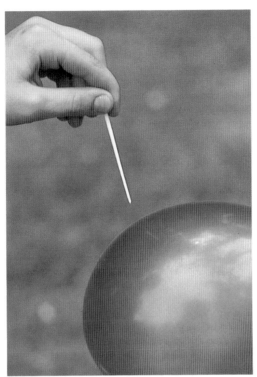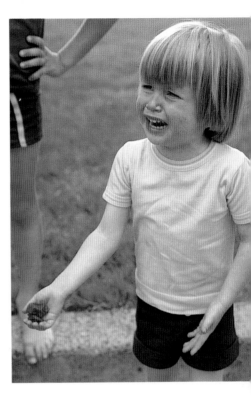

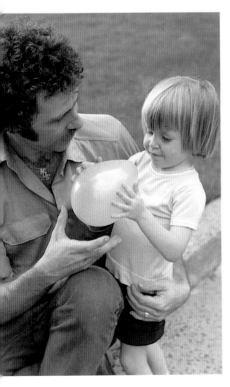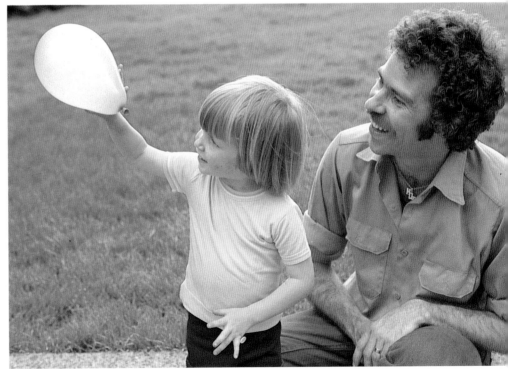

WHAT CHILDREN LEARN FROM TAKING PICTURES

In real life and in moving pictures so much happens so fast that children often wonder if they really saw what they saw. But the still photograph of that fleeting moment is there to look at many times, to savor, to remember.

Parents who encourage their children to take photographs give them an important message: that the life surrounding them is interesting, complex, and exciting. And that capturing people as they really are (not only as they pretend to be while being photographed) is worthwhile and important. Smiles are nice, but so are feeling sad because a pet has been hurt and being serious while studying a rock formation.

The world is full of subject matter. It is only a question of what to choose. And you need not travel to faraway places to get interesting pictures. Everyone around is trying to achieve something—what better subject matter? For instance, a child's baby sister or brother is learning something new nearly every day, and when that baby can first lift his or her head, the child sees that the delighted smile is certainly worth photographing. This is just the first of many photo opportunities for the older sibling.

Later, babies crawl, then try to learn to walk. They learn to tie their shoelaces. They try out new toys. They learn to speak, sing, dance, and play musical instruments. They do gymnastics and turn cartwheels; they participate in sports, too. They paint, draw, and sculpt. They learn to read, type, and even use a computer. They do their homework. They build with blocks and build sand castles. And they smile proudly when their achievements are acknowledged at home or by their classmates during show and tell.

If there is a new baby in the family or in a neighbor's family, children can decide to show the baby growing up by going back for another few shots every week or every month. What a wealth of physical and emotional growth to notice and learn about!

Many children only think of their parents as authority figures and care givers. How about being allowed to record them at work, playing in a tennis tournament, fishing, or riding on a merry-go-round with their other children? Through such shots, children will be able to see their parents as they really are—as human.

As we know, nothing can evoke meaningful memories as a photograph. Here is a mother, hugging her children after coming back from a trip. The next shot shows two friends during a bitter quarrel that made the photographer feel awful, and at the same time, glad that it was someone else's quarrel. Here is a little brother, holding his new baby sister, his face a peculiar mixture of happiness and jealousy. Then two years later, the tables have turned; now it is the little one's turn to be frustrated because she cannot climb up on a bed or do all the "grownup" things her brother can do.

If the children are lucky enough to know their grandparents, they can start a project recording the older generations way of life, including such hobbies as baking and woodworking. Later, they will remember having a special, appreciative relationship with and giving pleasure to their grandparents, and will have learned about their grandparents. The children will practically hear their relatives as they look at the photographs they have taken.

Finally, if children like cats and dogs, they can also chronicle the animals' lives, watch them grow up, give birth, and bring up their babies.

Yes, these are the things that give photography meaning. It is only natural that the pictures themselves should tell the story clearly with a simple but reliable technique. "Photography," after all, means "writing with light": you should not have to use words instead.

So, all potential photographers—children and adults alike—must spend some time learning to handle the camera, to determine when the available light is sufficient or when a flash is needed, to see whether the background needs a bit of cleaning up, to figure out if you can achieve this simply by standing on a chair or squatting on the floor, and so on. While it's true that instant cameras delight children, I must emphasize that giggling at the results is *not* the aim of photography. Showing the world as they see it *is* their goal. And when this is made clear from the start, children will want to learn, and fast.

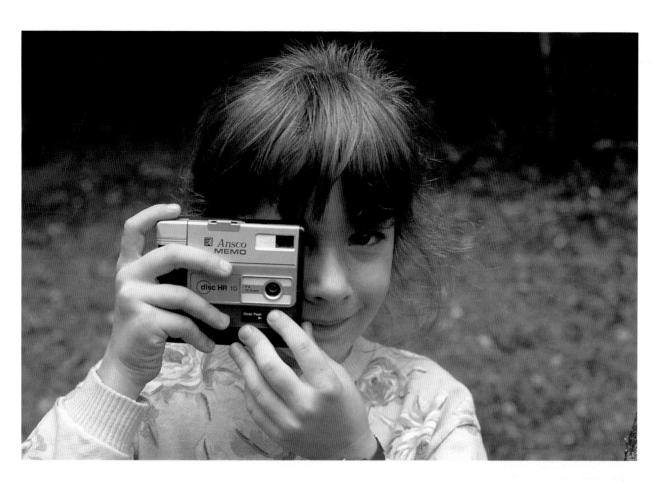

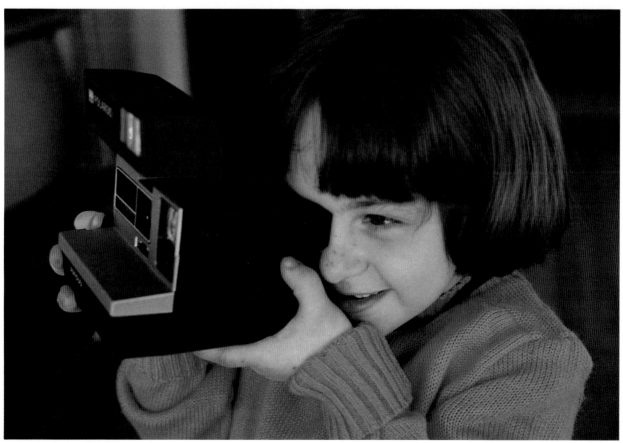

INDEX